FLORIDA CRIMINAL LAW 101

By
Darren W. Freeman

This book was written for any person who serves or will serve in any capacity of Law Enforcement in Florida to use as a guide to understand the Criminal Law Statues that are dealt with daily, by Florida Law Enforcement Officers. It's also for the average Person who wishes to gain a direct understanding and knowledge of certain Florida Criminal Law Violations and Statues.

It provides a good understanding of not just how the Statues are written, but also how they are interpreted and enforced. I have seen many great students graduate a Law Enforcement Academy and have great difficulty in applying what they learned in a book to real world application.

I have taken all the experience I have from teaching in Several Institutions of Higher Education from South Florida State College Criminal Justice Academy, to Polk State College Criminal Justice Academy, to Valencia College Criminal Justice Academy and the Criminal Justice Academy of Osceola (TECO), to assist me with writing this Book

The one area that I do love to teach is "Criminal Law".

So, I will be taking you through some of the Florida Criminal Law that I know you will be dealing with on a regular basis. I am going to teach you about the importance of the words **AND/OR**.

You will be learning how to apply what you read and learn to real world situations

This book will help not only to a learning process of the Law, but to also assist after you have graduated from a Law Enforcement Academy, a great prep prior to entering a law Enforcement Academy and a great resource before taking any Florida Law Enforcement Exams or Interview for a Florida Law Enforcement Career.

This book is **not** intended to give any reader Legal Advice. This book is designed from the

Authors Professional Florida Law Enforcement and Correctional Officer Experience and as a Certified Florida Department of Law Enforcement Instructor, and his Personal Professional Point of view as an Instructor and Teacher.

When reading and trying to interpret a Statue, you must be mindful of how the Statue is written. Statues come written in many different ways, and it will be up to you, to be able to first understand what your reading and then learn the elements of it and then be able to look at a situation and decide if a criminal act had occurred or not, and if it did occur what State Statue, County Ordinance or City Ordinance, if any, were violated by the individual(s) your dealing with.

Let's look at each Statue, County Ordinance and City Ordinance as a Cake Recipe. If all the elements are not there, then you **do not** have a Cake or a Crime.

This is where the words **"AND"** and **"OR",** come into play. When a Statue reads that for someone to be charged with this crime or violation, the person must have committed, this, **and** this, **and** this. So, there would be three things the person had to do to be charged with the violation of that Statue. So, like a Cake

Recipe, you might have the first part, the second part but not the third part or element. This means **no violation** of the Statue. So, if the person did have **all** the three elements, then Yes, the person can be charged with Violation of the Statue or Ordinance.

Now if the word **"OR"** is used, the Statue reads that someone to be charged with this crime or violation, they must have committed, This, **or** This, **or** This. So, this means if the individual violated **any one** of the three elements of this Statue, they can be charged with Violating the Statue.

Now let's say you read a statue that says if the person committed this one thing or only **1 element**, then they are in violation of the Statue or Ordinance. You investigate and conclude that this individual did commit the one element needed, then yes, a violation of the Statue or Ordinance occurred, and **you can** take enforcement action.

If there was **no violation** of **any** of the **elements** to any statue, or Ordinance your reviewing or considering, then you have **No Crime or Violation**.

This will become a lot clearer as we move forward into Florida Criminal Statues.

LET'S BEGIN!!

784.011   Assault

(1)   An "assault" is an intentional, unlawful threat by word or act to do violence to the person of another, coupled with an apparent ability to do so and doing some act which creates a well-founded fear in such other person that such violence is imminent. (2) Whoever commits an assault shall be guilty of a misdemeanor of the second degree.

(Read Assault Statue) See how the statue is broken down, Intentional Act, threat by word **or** act, against another person, with the ability to carry out the threat **or** act, which creates a well-founded fear that the act is imminent. Think of the word Assault as Insult. Assault the person **never** actually hits or strikes someone but does make the attempt.

SCENARIO 1: Billy walks up to Johnny in a parking lot. Billy tells Johnny that he is going to punch his face in. Johnny is afraid of Billy. Billy walks toward him and throws a punch missing him but caused Johnny to move and Johnny was in fear.

1, Billy was present and made a verbal threat.
2, This created a well-founded fear in Johnny.

3, Billy walked towards him and threw a punch. All the elements are there. **ASSAULT**

SCENARIO 2: Billy Calls Johnny on the Telephone. Billy tells Johnny that he is going to punch his face in when he sees him tomorrow at work. Johnny is afraid of Billy. This phone call put Johnny in fear, and he knows Billy can carry out the threat.

1, Billy did call Johnny and make a threat. 2, This created a well-founded fear in Johnny.

All the elements are there except for 1, There is no way for Billy to complete the Assault because it is over the phone. Billy has no way of carrying out his threat. Not Imminently or Immediately going to happen. Billy is at his home 3 miles away. **NO ASSAULT**

You must remember when you can, ask your victim if this crime was against their will and without their permission. You will be surprised when suspected victims will tell you "No I wasn't Scared, I told him to "bring it on" and he missed". This turns the alleged victim no longer a victim but an active participant, and no, longer a Victim of Assault.

784.021   Aggravated assault

(1)   An "aggravated assault" is an assault:

(a)   With a deadly weapon without intent to kill; or

(b)   With an intent to commit a felony.

(2)   Whoever commits an aggravated assault shall be guilty of a felony of the third degree,

(Read Aggravated Assault Statue) See how the statue is broken down, Intentional Act, threat by word **or** act, against another person, with the ability to carry out the threat **or** act, which creates a well-founded fear that the act is imminent. Think of the word Aggravated Assault as Insult but with a Weapon. Aggravated Assault just like simple Assault the person **never** actually hits or strikes someone but does make the attempt with a Weapon.

SCENARIO 1: Billy walks up to Johnny in a parking lot with a baseball bat. Billy tells Johnny that he is going to break his face with the Baseball bat. Johnny is afraid of Billy. Billy walks toward him and Swings the Bat missing Johnny's head. Johnny was in fear for his life and had to run from Billy to avoid being hit. Johnny was in total fear that he was going to be hit.

1, Billy was present and made a verbal threat. 2, Billy was holding a Base Ball bat and threatened to use it as a Weapon against Johnny. 3, This created a well-founded fear in Johnny that this was going to imminently happen. 3, Billy walked towards him and swung the bat at Johnny's head. All the elements are there. **AGGRAVATED ASSAULT**

SCENARIO 2: Billy Calls Johnny on the Telephone. Billy tells Johnny that he is going to beat hiss face in with a Base Ball Bat tomorrow at work. Johnny is afraid of Billy. This phone call put Johnny in fear, and he knows Billy can carry out the threat.

1, Billy did call Johnny and make a threat about using a Bat as a Weapon. 2, This created a well-founded fear in Johnny.

All the elements are there except for 1, There is no way for Billy to complete the AGGRAVATED Assault because it is over the phone. Billy has no way of carrying out his threat. Not Imminently or Immediately going to happen. Billy is at his home 3 miles away. **NO AGGRAVATED ASSAULT**

You must remember when you can, ask your victim if this crime was against their will and without their permission. You will be

surprised when suspected victims will tell you "No I wasn't scared, and I told him to "bring it on" and he missed". This turns the alleged victim no longer a victim but an active participant, and no, longer a Victim of Aggravated Assault.

784.03   Battery/Felony Battery

(1)(a)   The offense of battery occurs when a person:

1.   Actually, and intentionally touches or strikes another person against the will of the other; or

2.   Intentionally causes bodily harm to another person.

(b)   Except as provided in subsection (2), a person who commits battery commits a misdemeanor of the first degree, punishable as provided in s. 775.082 or s. 775.083.

(2)   A person who has one prior conviction for battery, aggravated battery, or felony battery and who commits any second or subsequent battery commits a felony of the third degree, punishable as provided in s. 775.082, s. 775.083, or s. 775.084. For purposes of this subsection, "conviction" means a determination of guilt that is the result of a plea or a trial, regardless of whether adjudication is withheld or a plea of nolo contendere is entered.

(Read Battery Statue) See how the statue is broken down, Intentional and Actually hits another person. This means that one individual went further than making a verbal threat and hit another person. Now Battery can be any touching or striking, this can be a punch, a push, a poke, a kick, hitting someone with an object like a book, a wooden Ruler etc. There are many variances to Battery on a person with the intention of causing some harm to another.

SCENARIO 1: Billy walks up to Johnny in a parking lot. Billy tells Johnny that he is going to punch his face in. Johnny is afraid of Billy. Johnny tells Billy that he doesn't want to Fight. Billy walks toward him and throws a punch hitting Johnny on his nose causing him to bleed and fall to the ground.

 1, Billy was present and made a verbal threat and carried it out by hitting Johnny. 2, This created a well-founded fear in Johnny. 3, Johnny was punched one time in his face. All the elements are there. **BATTERY**

SCENARIO 2: Billy walks up to Johnny in a parking lot. Billy tells Johnny that he is going to punch his face in. Johnny is afraid of Billy. Johnny tells Billy that he doesn't want to Fight. Billy walks toward him and throws a punch hitting Johnny on his nose causing him to bleed and fall to the ground. Billy then jumps on top of Johnny Punching him repeatedly breaking Johnny's Jaw.

1, Billy was present and made a verbal threat and carried it out by hitting Johnny. 2, This created a well-founded fear in Johnny. 3, Johnny was punched repeatedly in his face while Billy held him down Breaking Johnny's Jaw. All the elements are there. **FELONY BATTERY.**

Felony Battery was created for instances where great harm or disfigurement did occur to the victim, but the Attacker did not use an Actual Weapon or Object to cause the harm, as is used in an Aggravated Battery where a Weapon is used to cause harm.

You must remember when you can, ask your victim if this crime was against their will and without their permission. You will be surprised when suspected victims will tell you "No I wasn't Scared, and I told him to "bring it on", "I was ready to Fight him". This turns the alleged victim no longer a victim but an active participant, and no, longer a Victim of Battery or Felony Battery.

784.041   Felony battery/domestic battery by strangulation

(1)   A person commits felony battery if he or she:

(a)   Actually and intentionally touches or strikes another person against the will of the other; and

(b)   Causes great bodily harm, permanent disability, or permanent disfigurement.

(2)(a)   A person commits domestic battery by strangulation if the person knowingly and intentionally, against the will of another, impedes the normal breathing or circulation of the blood of a family or household member or of a person with whom he or she is in a dating relationship, so as to create a risk of or cause great bodily harm by applying pressure on the throat or neck of the other person or by blocking the nose or mouth of the other person. This paragraph does not apply to any act of medical diagnosis, treatment, or prescription which is authorized under the laws of this state.

(b)   As used in this subsection, the term:

1. "Family or household member" has the same meaning as in s. 741.28.

2. "Dating relationship" means a continuing and significant relationship of a romantic or intimate nature.

(3) A person who commits felony battery or domestic battery by strangulation commits a felony of the third degree, punishable as provided in s. 775.082, s. 775.083, or s. 775.084.

(Read Felony Battery and Domestic Violence Statue) See how the statue is broken down, Intentional and Actually hits another person. This means that one individual went further than making a verbal threat and hit another person. Now Battery can be any touching or striking, this can be a punch, a push, a poke, a kick, hitting someone with an object like a book, a wooden Ruler etc. There are many variances to Battery on a person with the intention of causing some harm to another. The difference here is in Florida if you have someone who has Committed Domestic Violence Battery. Then that person needs to be arrested and charged accordingly.

Domestic Relationship is described like this; Hitting A Family Member, Mom, Dad, Sister Brother etc. This would also include any Blood Relatives First Cousins, Grandparents. Stepbrothers and Stepsisters, any person who has lived with another person as if a Family unit at one time or another OR have a Child in common. If two people have a child together whether they ever lived together or not, it would be Battery Domestic Violence because of the relationship of sharing their child.

A **Boyfriend** and **Girlfriend** who have **No Child** Together and have **never lived** Together as a Family Unit, and who are **not related** by blood or Marriage, Should **Strike** and **Batter** Each Other, would **<u>NOT BE</u>** "Battery Domestic Violence", it would be just **Simple Battery.**

SCENARIO 1: Billy walks up to his Dad in a parking lot. Billy tells His Dad that he is going to punch his face in. Dad is afraid of Billy. Dad tells Billy that he doesn't want to Fight. Billy walks toward him and throws a punch hitting his Dad on his nose causing him to bleed and fall to the ground.

1, Billy was present and made a verbal threat and carried it out by hitting his Dad. 2, This created a well-founded fear in his Dad. 3, His Dad was punched one time in his face. 4, The

Family Relationship exists because they are Father and Son. All the elements are there. **BATTERY DOMESTIC VIOLENCE. It does not matter where the Battery Occurs, in the Home or in a Shopping Parking lot.**

SCENARIO 2: Billy walks up to his Dad in a parking lot. Billy tells his Dad, that he is going to punch his face in. His dad is afraid of Billy. His Dad tells his son Billy that he doesn't want to Fight. Billy walks toward him and throws a punch hitting his Dad on his nose causing him to bleed and fall to the ground. Billy **then** jumps on top of his Dad Punching him repeatedly breaking his Dad's Jaw.

1, Billy was present and made a verbal threat and carried it out by hitting his Dad. 2, This created a well-founded fear in his Dad. 3, His Dad was punched repeatedly in his face while Billy held him down Breaking his Dad's Jaw. All the elements are there. **FELONY BATTERY DOMESTIC VIOLENCE**

Felony Battery was created for instances where great harm or disfigurement did occur to the victim, but the Attacker did not use an Actual Weapon or Object to cause the harm, as is used in an Aggravated Battery where a Weapon is used to cause harm.

You must remember when it comes to any charge of Criminal Domestic Violence, you must have a Crime against a person as outlined. A husband or Wife who runs out to the Family Car and smashes the window, is not an act of Criminal Domestic Violence. Screaming at each other inside a home also not an act of Criminal Domestic Violence. Walking into a home that was destroyed by one spouse is also not Criminal Domestic Violence. It must be a Physical Criminal Act for this Statue.

It does not matter if the Victim wants to press charges or not. If you have all the elements then it does not matter, you are acting as the State Stepping in and Charging one or more persons involved in the physical altercation. You can ask your victim if this crime was against their will and without their permission. You will be surprised when victims will tell you that it wasn't and that they do not want to press charges. As I stated it doesn't matter whether they do or don't, want to follow through with the Criminal Charges, that will be decided by your State Attorney's Office. Make the Arrest if YOU HAVE ALL THE ELEMENTS!

784.045   Aggravated Battery

(1)(a)   A person commits aggravated battery who, in committing battery:

1.   Intentionally or knowingly causes great bodily harm, permanent disability, or permanent disfigurement or

2.   Uses a deadly weapon.

(b)   A person commits aggravated battery if the person who was the victim of the battery was pregnant at the time of the offense and the offender knew or should have known that the victim was pregnant.

(2)   Whoever commits aggravated battery shall be guilty of a felony of the second degree, punishable as provided in s. 775.082, s. 775.083, or s. 775.084.

(Read Aggravated Battery Statue) See how the statue is broken down, Intentional and Actually hits another person. This means that one individual went further than making a verbal threat and hit another person and used a WEAPON to do it. Aggravated Battery is an Intentional act against another person to Cause

Great Harm to that person, and in doing so a WEAPON was used to cause that Harm.

SCENARIO 1: Billy walks up to Johnny in a parking lot with a baseball bat. Billy tells Johnny that he is going to break his face with the Baseball bat. Johnny is afraid of Billy. Billy walks toward him and Swings the Bat Hitting Johnny in his Face with the Bat. This Caused Johnny to have a Broken Jaw, and Broken Nose. **(A Baseball Bat by Design is not a Weapon, BUT when a person uses the Bat to Beat, Strike OR Threaten Someone with it, they have now turned it into a "Weapon")**

1, Billy was present and made a verbal threat. 2, Billy was holding a Base Ball bat and threatened to use it as a Weapon against Johnny. 3, Billy went at Johnny with the Bat Striking him in the Face, causing a broken Jaw and Nose. 3, Johnny did not want to Fight Billy. 4, Billy intended to cause great harm to Johnny. Are all the Elements there? **YES,** All the elements are there. **AGGRAVATED BATTERY with a WEAPON**

784.08 Assault or battery on persons 65 years of age or older/ reclassification of offenses/ minimum sentence

(1)　A person who is convicted of an aggravated assault or aggravated battery upon a person 65 years of age or older shall be sentenced to a minimum term of imprisonment of 3 years and fined not more than $10,000 and shall also be ordered by the sentencing judge to make restitution to the victim of such offense and to perform up to 500 hours of community service work. Restitution and community service work shall be in addition to any fine or sentence which may be imposed and shall not be in lieu thereof.

(2)　Whenever a person is charged with committing an assault or aggravated assault or a battery or aggravated battery upon a person 65 years of age or older, regardless of whether he or she knows or has reason to know the age of the victim, the offense for which the person is charged shall be reclassified as follows:

(a)   In the case of aggravated battery, from a felony of the second degree to a felony of the first degree.

(b)   In the case of aggravated assault, from a felony of the third degree to a felony of the second degree.

(c)   In the case of battery, from a misdemeanor of the first degree to a felony of the third degree.

(d)   In the case of assault, from a misdemeanor of the second degree to a misdemeanor of the first degree.

(3)   Notwithstanding the provisions of s. 948.01, adjudication of guilt or imposition of sentence shall not be suspended, deferred, or withheld.

(Read the Assault or Battery on Persons 65 years or Older) This Statue mirrors what we have already read involving Assault or battery and the Elements needed to charge a person Criminally. Everything is the same, EXCEPT if the Victim is 65 Years of Age or Older. Committing an act of Physical Violence in this Statue enhances the Actual Charge. It basically upgrades the actual charge by one degree, Like a Simple Battery from a Misdemeanor of the

First Degree to Automatically a "Felony" of the Third Degree. One aspect of charging this is if the Victim as noted is 65 years old or older.

784.07 Assault or battery of law enforcement officers, firefighters, emergency medical care providers, public transit employees or agents, or other specified officers/ reclassification of offenses/ minimum sentences

(1) As used in this section, the term:

(a) "Emergency medical care provider" means an ambulance driver, emergency medical technician, paramedic, registered nurse, physician as defined in s. 401.23, medical director as defined in s. 401.23, or any person authorized by an emergency medical service licensed under chapter 401 who is engaged in the performance of his or her duties. The term "emergency medical care provider" also includes physicians, employees, agents, or volunteers of hospitals as defined in chapter 395, who are employed, under contract, or otherwise authorized by a hospital to perform duties directly associated with the care and treatment rendered by the hospital's emergency department or the security thereof.

(b)   "Firefighter" means any person employed by any public employer of this state whose duty it is to extinguish fires; to protect life or property; or to enforce municipal, county, and state fire prevention codes, as well as any law pertaining to the prevention and control of fires.

(c)   "Law enforcement explorer" means any person who is a current member of a law enforcement agency's explorer program and who is performing functions other than those required to be performed by sworn law enforcement officers on behalf of a law enforcement agency while under the direct physical supervision of a sworn officer of that agency and wearing a uniform that bears at least one patch that clearly identifies the law enforcement agency that he or she represents.

(d)   "Law enforcement officer" includes a law enforcement officer, a correctional officer, a correctional probation officer, a part-time law enforcement officer, a part-time correctional officer, an auxiliary law enforcement officer, and an auxiliary correctional officer, as those terms are respectively defined in s. 943.10, and any county probation officer; an employee or agent of the Department of Corrections who supervises or provides services to inmates; an officer of the Florida Commission on Offender Review; a federal law enforcement officer as defined in s. 901.1505; and law enforcement personnel of the Fish and Wildlife Conservation Commission, the Department of Environmental Protection, or the Department of Law Enforcement.

(Read the Assault or Battery on Law Enforcement Officers and Others) This Statue mirrors what we have already read involving Assault or battery and the Elements needed to charge a person Criminally. Everything is the same, EXCEPT if the Victim is Law Enforcement Officer or Others outlined in the Statue and a Criminal Act of Violence is done against one of them while on "**DUTY".** Committing an act of Physical Violence in this Statue enhances the Actual Charge. It basically upgrades the actual charge by one degree, Like a Simple Battery from a Misdemeanor of the First Degree to Automatically a "Felony" of the Third Degree.

776.012   Use or threatened use of force in defense of person

(1)   A person is justified in using or threatening to use force, except deadly force, against another when and to the extent that the person reasonably believes that such conduct is necessary to defend himself or herself or another against the other's imminent use of unlawful force. A person who uses or threatens to use force in accordance with this subsection does not have a duty to retreat before using or threatening to use such force.

(2)   A person is justified in using or threatening to use deadly force if he or she reasonably believes that using or threatening to use such force is necessary to prevent imminent death or great bodily harm to himself or herself or another or to prevent the imminent commission of a forcible felony. A person who uses or threatens to use deadly force in accordance with this subsection does not have a duty to retreat and has the right to stand his

or her ground if the person using or threatening to use the deadly force is not engaged in a criminal activity and is in a place where he or she has a right to be.

(Read the Use or threatened us of Force in defense of a person) This Statue is obvious. Some might say its self-explanatory. A person can use threatened harm or physical harm against another person from causing harm to themselves or another.   Ok, a person can defend themselves. Judgment in this area as to what is defending oneself to committing a crime themselves.

SCENARIO: If Billy starts a Fist fight with Johnny, and Johnny does not want to fight, BUT decides to Stand His Ground and Fight Billy, he does **not** need to retreat. Johnny only used enough Force to make Billy Back away. Can this be Justifiable Force by Johnny? YES, it can be.

SCENARIO: Billy is standing in the middle of a shopping plaza screaming that he wants to beat someone and attacks a Female Shopper Walking to her car and starts to Punch and Kick her. Johnny sees this and runs over to Billy and throws him to the Ground to get him away from the Female. Johnny has to strike and punch Billy to try and Control him. He and Billy are the same size. Johnny only uses enough force to get control over Billy. Johnny holds Billy on the ground until Law Enforcement Arrives. Can this be Justifiable Force by Johnny? YES, it can.

SCENARIO: Billy goes to the Local Movie Theater upset over a certain movie playing and he decides to take out his 9mm Pistol and starts shooting at people. Johnny runs to his car and pulls out his 357 Magnum Revolver and shoots at Billy. Billy and Johnny exchange gun Fire. Johnny Kills Billy. Can this use of force by Johnny be Justifiable? YES, it can be Justifiable Use of Deadly force in defense of oneself and others.

SCENARIO: Billy pulls up in a Parking lot and starts to Argue with Johnny over a Parking Space. Billy grabs a Knife and charges Johnny. Johnny has no Weapon, and this was a sudden attack, so Johnny punches at Billy striking him in the throat. Billy falls and dies because his windpipe was crushed. Can this use of force by Johnny be Justifiable? **YES,** this can be.

Any use of force must be judged by many factors, including the size of the person that force is being used to stop their Violent Actions.

SCENARIO: Bobby is in a shopping parking lot and starts yelling and tries to hit another shopper in the parking lot. The shopper he is trying to hit with his fist is Michael a 25-year-old 6,1' 250-pound Body Builder and Bobby is 5-foot-tall 115 pound 86 year old male with a walker. Michael grabs Bobby and slams him to the ground and starts punching him repeatedly until Bobby passes out. Can this be Justifiable Use of Force? Probably NOT. Did Michael have to use such force to control Bobby? Probably NOT. Could Michael be looking at Criminal Charges? Probably Most Definitely.

You must be justified in the use of force you use against another even when defending yourself or another from Harm. Controlling Force is fine. If the person there is trying to stop, STOPs and gives up its over. A person is not Justified to Continue further Force if the threat is stopped.

776.031   Use or threatened use of force in defense of property

(1)   A person is justified in using or threatening to use force, except deadly force, against another when and to the extent that the person reasonably believes that such conduct is necessary to prevent or terminate the other's trespass on, or other tortious or criminal interference with, either real property other than a dwelling or personal property, lawfully in his or her possession or in the possession of another who is a member of his or her immediate family or household or of a person whose property he or she has a legal duty to protect. A person who uses or threatens to use force in accordance with this subsection does not have a duty to retreat before using or threatening to use such force.

(2)   A person is justified in using or threatening to use deadly force only if he or she reasonably believes that such conduct is necessary to prevent the imminent commission of a forcible felony. A person who uses or threatens to use deadly force in accordance

with this subsection does not have a duty to retreat and has the right to stand his or her ground if the person using or threatening to use the deadly force is not engaged in a criminal activity and is in a place where he or she has a right to be.

(Read Home Protection and use of Force). This Statute covers everything you already have read in 776.012, Justifiable use of Force. The only thing different is that these crimes are occurring in Someone's Occupied Home, Occupied Vehicle, Dwelling or Residence, and the Occupants are in Fear of Imminent Violence against them.

In Florida it is still Considered, that a person's home is there Castle. If an intruder were to enter by force a home with intent to commit a crime in that home including a violent crime against the occupants in the home, then any and all Force would be Justifiable if the occupants Feared for their Safety and Feared that they would or could become the victim of Death or Serious Bodily Harm OR someone else in the home could be a Victim to Physical harm and attack.

776.032 Immunity from criminal prosecution and civil action for justifiable use or threatened use of force

(1)   A person who uses or threatens to use force as permitted in s. 776.012, s. 776.013, or s. 776.031 is justified in such conduct and is immune from criminal prosecution and civil action for the use or threatened use of such force by the person, personal representative, or heirs of the person against whom the force was used or threatened, unless the person against whom force was used or threatened is a law enforcement officer, as defined in s. 943.10(14), who was acting in the performance of his or her official duties and the officer identified himself or herself in accordance with any applicable law or the person using or threatening to use force knew or reasonably should have known that the person was a law enforcement officer. As used in this subsection, the term "criminal prosecution" includes arresting, detaining in custody, and charging or prosecuting the defendant.

(2)   A law enforcement agency may use standard procedures for investigating the use or threatened use of force as described in subsection (1), but the agency may not arrest the person for using or threatening to use force unless it determines that there is probable cause that the force that was used or threatened was unlawful.

(3)   The court shall award reasonable attorney's fees, court costs, compensation for loss of income, and all expenses incurred by the defendant in defense of any civil action brought by a plaintiff if the court finds that the defendant is immune from prosecution as provided in subsection (1).

(4)   In a criminal prosecution, once a prima facie claim of self-defense immunity from criminal prosecution has been raised by the defendant at a pretrial immunity hearing, the burden of proof by clear and convincing evidence is on the party seeking to overcome the immunity from criminal prosecution provided in subsection (1).

(Read Immunity from use of Force). This Statute covers everything you already have read in 776.032, This falls under the direct use of Force or Threatened for a person uses against another. If any person uses force in defense of himself or another, and it was shown to be necessary and reasonable considering the circumstances, then that person will be exempt from Criminal and/or Civil Prosecution.

776.041   Use or threatened use of force by aggressor The justification described in the preceding sections of this chapter is not available to a person who:

(1)   Is attempting to commit, committing, or escaping after the commission of, a forcible felony or

(2)   Initially provokes the use or threatened use of force against himself or herself, unless:

(a)   Such force or threat of force is so great that the person reasonably believes that he or she is in imminent danger of death or great bodily harm and that he or she has exhausted every reasonable means to escape such danger other than the use or threatened use of force which is likely to cause death or great bodily harm to the assailant or

(b)   In good faith, the person withdraws from physical contact with the assailant and indicates clearly to the assailant that he or she desires to withdraw and terminate the use or threatened use of force, but the assailant continues or resumes the use or threatened use of force.

(Read Use or threatened use of force by aggressor). This Statute covers an aggressor's use of Force against another.   The aggressor has no safeguards form Criminal or Civil Prosecution for their actions.

776.05   Law enforcement officers/ use of force in making an arrest A law enforcement officer, or any person whom the officer has summoned or directed to assist him or her, need not retreat or desist from efforts to make a lawful arrest because of resistance or threatened resistance to the arrest. The officer is justified in the use of any force:

(1)   Which he or she reasonably believes to be necessary to defend himself or herself or another from bodily harm while making the arrest,

(2)   When necessarily committed in retaking felons who have escaped or

(3)   When necessarily committed in arresting felons fleeing from justice. However, this subsection shall not constitute a defense in any civil action for damages brought for the wrongful use of deadly force unless the use of deadly force was necessary to prevent the arrest from being defeated by such flight and, when feasible, some warning had been given, and:

(a)   The officer reasonably believes that the fleeing felon poses a threat of death or serious physical harm to the officer or others or

(b)   The officer reasonably believes that the fleeing felon has committed a crime involving the infliction or threatened infliction of serious physical harm to another person.

(Read Law Enforcement Officers use of Force in making an arrest). This Statute covers all Florida Law Enforcement Officers in all Branches of Law Enforcement. In making an arrest a Law Enforcement Officer can use any and all force necessary to make a Lawful Legal Arrest, BUT the Force must be needed and is reasonable. The standard would be, would another Law Enforcement Officer have used the same force in the same situation. You must be justified in any Force when arresting any Individual. You are not EXEMPT from Prosecution for Using Excessive and unnecessary Force against a person. If it is discovered that the Law Enforcement Officer Used excessive and unnecessary Force, that Officer can be looking at Criminal and Civil Prosecution. ALWAYS approach any situation as if you are on CAMERA.

776.051 Use or threatened use of force in resisting arrest or making an arrest or in the execution of a legal duty/ prohibition

(1)   A person is not justified in the use or threatened use of force to resist an arrest by a law enforcement officer, or to resist a law enforcement officer who is engaged in the execution of a legal duty, if the law enforcement officer was acting in good faith and he or she is known, or reasonably appears, to be a law enforcement officer.

(2)   A law enforcement officer, or any person whom the officer has summoned or directed to assist him or her, is not justified in the use of force if the arrest or execution of a legal duty is unlawful and known by him or her to be unlawful.

(Read Use or Threatened use of force in resisting arrest). This Statute covers when a law Enforcement Officer is making an arrest, that the arrestee has no right to physically resist or use force to stop the Officer from making a Legal Arrest. The arrest must be Lawful, and the Officer must be acting in Good Faith in determining the Arrest to be Lawful. It is unlawful for an Officer to make an arrest **knowing** that the arrest is not Lawful and Justified.

776.06 Deadly force by a law enforcement or correctional officer

(1)   As applied to a law enforcement officer or correctional officer acting in the performance of his or her official duties, the term "deadly force" means force that is likely to cause death or great bodily harm and includes, but is not limited to:

(a)   The firing of a firearm in the direction of the person to be arrested, even though no intent exists to kill or inflict great bodily harm; and

(b)   The firing of a firearm at a vehicle in which the person to be arrested is riding.

(2)(a)   The term "deadly force" does not include the discharge of a firearm by a law enforcement officer or correctional officer during and within the scope of his or her official duties which is loaded with a less-lethal munition. As used in this subsection, the term "less-lethal munition" means a projectile that is designed to stun, temporarily incapacitate, or cause temporary discomfort to a person without penetrating the person's body.

(b)   A law enforcement officer or a correctional officer is not liable in any civil or criminal action arising out of the use of any less-lethal munition in good faith during and within the scope of his or her official duties.

(Read Deadly use of Force). This Statute covers Law Enforcement and Correctional Officers. Deadly Force is the last resort for an Officer to have to use. To use deadly force an Officer needs to be in Clear Fear for their Lives or another's life in using Deadly Force.   That the Aggressor's actions posed a serious likely hood that they would cause death or great bodily harm to the Officer or Another. This would also mean an "Immediate" threat. The shooting of a Firearm at a Suspect is the Use of Deadly Force whether you strike the Suspect or Not.

There has been some confusion with certain law Enforcement Agencies that make Officers write reports for use of Force when all they did was draw their weapon and point it towards a Suspect or Suspects. THIS IS **NOT A USE OF FORCE**. YOU ARE ONLY CREATING A HEIGHTENED PRESENCE OF YOUR AUTHORITY. Use of Force is just that, FORCE WAS USED, pointing a gun isn't, unless the Officer pulls the trigger. <u>YOU ARE NOT ALLOWED TO USE DEADLY FORCE AGAINST SOMEONE COMMITTING A PROPERTY CRIME.</u>

<u>SCENARIO:</u> Officer Bob is at Billy bad Boys House on a Domestic Violence Call. Officer Bob knocks at the Front Door, and Billy swings open the door pointing his Rifle at Officer Bob. Billy says he's going to shoot Officer Bob. Officer Bob draws his Firearm and shoots Billy three times Killing Billy. Justifiable? YES.

SCENARIO: Officer Bob gets a call of someone breaking into a car in a Shopping Plaza Parking lot. Officer Bob finds the Vehicle and the Suspect trying to hot wire the car. The Driver's side window was smashed out and the Suspect was trying to get into the steering wheel. Officer Bob watching this approaches the Suspect and gives verbal commands to the suspect to exit the vehicle with his hands up. The suspect follows Officer Bob's Commands. The Suspect then starts to run away, Officer Bob tells him to stop running. Suspects keeps running and Officer Bob Shoots the Suspect. Justified? NO   In this scenario the suspect never committed any type of Violent Person Crime. His crime would be that of a Property Crime, which would not justify that use of Force by Officer Bob.

776.07   Use of force to prevent escape

(1)   A law enforcement officer or other person who has an arrested person in his or her custody is justified in the use of any force which he or she reasonably believes to be necessary to prevent the escape of the arrested person from custody.

(2)   A correctional officer or other law enforcement officer is justified in the use of force, including deadly force, which he or she reasonably believes to be necessary to prevent the escape from a penal institution of a person whom the officer reasonably believes to be lawfully detained in such institution under sentence for an offense or awaiting trial or commitment for an offense.

(Read Use of Force to prevent Escape). This Statute reviews the authority of law Enforcement Officers and Correctional Officers that are authorized to use force in preventing the escape of an Incarcerated individual who has just been arrest or is currently incarcerated in a penal institution which would be any County or City Jail, or State Prison. All Officers still need to be mindful of the type of use of Force they are going to use to apprehend or stop the escape. The person escaping and the officer engaging needs to know or consider Public Safety should this escapee get back into the Public. Is the Person a Murder Suspect, A sexual Battery Suspect, Petit Thief etc. Does the use of force your about to do or attempt out way the Safety of the Public Should this Individual get away? Does this individual pose a DIRECT THREAT to the public? These are the questions that will be asked by what I call "Sideline Quarterbacks", which are usually Administrative Staff at your agency or your State Attorney's Office, especially if an Officer Uses DEADLY FORCE.

776.08   Forcible felony "Forcible felony" means treason, murder, manslaughter, sexual battery, carjacking, home-invasion robbery, robbery, burglary, arson, kidnapping, aggravated assault, aggravated battery, aggravated stalking, aircraft piracy, unlawful throwing, placing, or discharging of a destructive device or bomb, and any other felony which involves the use or threat of physical force or violence against any individual.

(Read Home Protection and use of Force). This Statute covers everything you already have read in 776.012, Justifiable use of Force. The only thing different is that these crimes are occurring in Someone's Occupied Home, Occupied Vehicle, Dwelling or Residence, and the Occupants are in Fear of Imminent Violence against them.

PRINCIPAL/ ACCESSORY/ ATTEMPT/ SOLICITATION/ CONSPIRACY

777.011   Principal in the first degree Whoever commits any criminal offense against the state, whether felony or misdemeanor, or aids, abets, counsels, hires, or otherwise procures such offense to be committed, and such offense is committed or is attempted to be committed, is a principal in the first degree and may be charged, convicted, and punished as such, whether he or she is or is not actually or constructively present at the commission of such offense.

(Read Principal in the first Degree). This Statute covers a principal in the First Degree. This includes anyone person who commits a Misdemeanor or Felony Crime. It also includes people that have assisted with the planning, execution or supplying services or other items to assist another to commit a crime. Whether they benefited from it or not. That person can be charged whether they are there physically or not with the same charge as the person who committed the crime or attempt to commit the crime.

SCENARIO: Billy gets his Friend Mike to drive a car for him while he robs at Gun Point the Manager at a local Liquor Store. Mike knows what Billy is doing and is outside in the car with the car running. Billy shoots and kills the Manager and runs from the store to Mike waiting in the car. Mike drives Billy away from the scene. Billy is arrested and charged with Murder. Mikes defense was that he was just in the car and assisted only by driving the car. Sorry Mike, according to this Statue you are being charged with Billy for the same Crime as Murder and you will be considered a Principal in the First Degree.

777.03   Accessory after the fact

(1)(a)   Any person not standing in the relation of husband or wife, parent or grandparent, child or grandchild, brother or sister, by consanguinity or affinity to the offender, who maintains or assists the principal or an accessory before the fact, or gives the offender any other aid, knowing that the offender had committed a crime and such crime was a third degree felony, or had been an accessory thereto before the fact, with the intent that the offender avoids or escapes detection, arrest, trial, or punishment, is an accessory after the fact.

(b)   Any person who maintains or assists the principal or accessory before the fact, or gives the offender any other aid, knowing that the offender had committed the offense of child abuse, neglect of a child, aggravated child abuse, aggravated manslaughter of a child under 18 years of age, or murder of a child under 18 years of age, or had been an accessory thereto before the fact, with the intent that the offender avoids or escapes detection, arrest, trial, or punishment, is an accessory after the fact unless the court finds that the person is a victim of domestic violence.

(c)   Any person who maintains or assists the principal or an accessory before the fact, or gives the offender any other aid, knowing that the offender had committed a crime and such crime was a capital, life, first degree, or second degree felony, or had been an accessory thereto before the fact, with the intent that the offender avoids or escapes detection, arrest, trial, or punishment, is an accessory after the fact.

(Read Accessory after the Fact). This Statute reviews the accessory after the fact crime. In the previous Statue it was discussed a Principal in the First Degree. This Statue is for persons who assist after the fact, which means they assist the Principal to conceal what they did, our are involved with giving aid and helping the Suspect hide from Law Enforcement. This is an Intentional act to help the Suspect with avoiding capture, or destruction of Evidence.

SCENARIO: Billy just robbed the Manager at Gun Point of the local Liquor Store. Billy runs to his Friends House Where his friend Steven Lives. He tells Steven what he did, and Steven hides Billy at his House. Officer Bob gets Dispatched to the Robbery. He recognizes Billy from Surveillance cameras from the Store. Officer Bob knows that Steven is a Friend of Billy's. He drives to Steve's House. He contacts Steve. He tells Steve what had occurred and that he is looking for Billy, and he wanted to know if he knew where Billy was. Steven Lies to Officer Bob and tells him he does not know anything about a Robbery and that Billy was not there.

Can Steven now be considered an Accessory after the Fact? **YES.**

SCENARIO: Billy just Robbed and Killed an Elderly man who was using an ATM machine in a shopping Plaza. Billy heads over to his Girlfriend Alexis House and gives her the gun he used to shoot the elderly man and a jacket he was wearing that was covered in the elderly man's blood. Alexis didn't know that Billy was going to commit this crime, but since she loves him, she takes the gun and throws it into a local lake for him to get rid of the Gun and burned the Coat up that Billy had been wearing. Can Alexis be an Accessory After the Fact? **YES.**

777.201   Entrapment

(1)   A law enforcement officer, a person engaged in cooperation with a law enforcement officer, or a person acting as an agent of a law enforcement officer perpetrates an entrapment if, for the purpose of obtaining evidence of the commission of a crime, he or she induces or encourages and, as a direct result, causes another person to engage in conduct constituting such crime by employing methods of persuasion or inducement which create a substantial risk that such crime will be committed by a person other than one who is ready to commit it.

(2)   A person prosecuted for a crime shall be acquitted if the person proves by a preponderance of the evidence that his or her criminal conduct occurred as a result of an entrapment. The issue of entrapment shall be tried by the trier of fact.

(Read Entrapment). This Statute reviews Entrapment. As a Law Enforcement Officer this is the statue that you need to be aware of.   In this Statue a person only needs to show a PREPONDERANCE of evidence to show they were a VICTIM of Entrapment by the law Enforcement Officer and Its Agency. That is how it would be documented in a Complaint against you and your Agency. If it is found that you did ENTRAPE a Person into committing a crime, your Case is done, and you can be subject depending on the Gravity of it, to Criminal Charges, Civil Tort Action against you and your agency, and Interdepartmental Disciplinary Charges.

SCENARIO: Sergeant Porter, Officer Smith, Officer Grant, Officer Nobry, and Officer Jones, are working an undercover prostitution Sting. Officer Smith is a Female Officer and is working undercover as a Prostitute. They Set up their operations in a part of their City where Prostitution is a problem. Officer Smith is standing out on a street corner and she sees a Black BMW stopped next to her at a Traffic light. SHE walks over to the vehicle and gestures the drive to lower his window, which he does. She then starts to engage with him asking if he would like to have a good time with her. The Driver asks, "What kind of Good Time?", She tells him that if he pulls over to the open parking lot next to her that she would have sex with him for $50.00 Dollars. So, the

Driver pulls into the Parking Lot where he is Arrested for Soliciting Prostitution. Can this be ENTRAPEMENT? **YES.**

You need to remember who initiated contact? Who talked about Sex? Who talked about money for sex? The answers to these questions are Officer Smith did. The driver would have to already be "predisposed" to committing this crime. The driver would have to be of a mindset that he was driving around looking to pay for sex from someone. The driver in this situation was **not** looking for a paid Sexual encounter BUT was **induced** and **encouraged** by Officer Smith to commit this Crime.

You cannot Create a CRIME to charge someone with a Crime.

CHAPTER 782
HOMICIDE

782.02   Justifiable use of deadly force The use of deadly force is justifiable when a person is resisting any attempt to murder such person or to commit any felony upon him or her or upon or in any dwelling house in which such person shall be.

(Read Justifiable use of Deadly Force). This Statute reviews the Justifiable use of Deadly Force. Deadly force can be used against another if the person is trying to cause the death or great Bodily harm to a person.

SCENARIO: Billy is a very jealous Ex-Boyfriend. He has been following his ex-girlfriend Peggy. Billy stops Peggy as she is walking into her apartment. He starts to yell at her and grabs her and throws her to the ground. Billy is 6 1'" 220 pounds. Peggy is 5 4" 110 pounds. Billy gets on top of her and starts to strangle her. Peggy feels she is going to die. Peggy manages to reach to her purse and pulls a Firearm out and shoots Billy off her. She shoots Billy 4 times and kills him. Can this be Justifiable? **YES.**

SCENARIO: Billy is going out with two friends to do a home Burglary. Billy carries a gun with him in case they are confronted by anyone in the home. It is 3am and Billy sees a home that he wants to enter to steal property. Billy and his two-friends pry open a kitchen window and crawl into the home. The two other friends with Billy do not have guns but are with him to commit this crime. The Homeowner wakes up and hears something in his Kitchen. He walks downstairs with his Gun that he keeps in his Bedroom. When he turns on the kitchen light, he sees Billy and his two friends. Billy pulls his gun out and points it at the Homeowner. The homeowner starts to Fire his gun at Billy and the other two men with Billy. Billy and the other two men are killed by the Homeowner. Can the Homeowner be Justified in shooting Billy? **YES.** Can the Homeowner be justified in the shooting of the other two men? **YES.** Billy's Friends are Principals in the First Degree with Billy.

782.03   Excusable homicide Homicide is excusable when committed by accident and misfortune in doing any lawful act by lawful means with usual ordinary caution, and without any unlawful intent, or by accident and misfortune in the heat of passion, upon any sudden and sufficient provocation, or upon a sudden combat, without any dangerous weapon being used and not done in a cruel or unusual manner.

(Read Excusable Homicide). This Statute reviews the Excusable homicide. These would be incidents where the perpetrator did not mean to kill a person, in each situation.

SCENARIO: Billy is high on METH. He decides that he wants to fight someone anyone. Billy leaves his home and starts walking down his block. Billy sees a guy jogging on the sidewalk. As the Jogger gets closer to Billy, Billy jumps Infront of the jogger and starts punching and kicking at the Jogger, the jogger punches at Billy and knocks Billy to the Ground. Billy hits his head on the Concrete and Dies from the Blow to his head. Can this be Excusable Homicide for the Jogger? **YES**

The jogger above was attacked suddenly. The Sudden Combat would be an Excusable Homicide Defense.

SCENARIO: Billy is with his Girlfriend Peggy. Peggy initiates a Sexual Encounter with Billy. They are at Peggy's Home. While they are engaged Sexually, Billy has a heart attack and dies. Can this be Excusable Homicide? **YES.**

782.04   Murder

782.07   Manslaughter

The Statutes of Murder and Manslaughter are broad. The best way to explain both statues is to incorporate them in general scenarios below.

Murder is by premeditated design. What I mean is that for Murder to be charged there must be premeditation to kill someone or a certain person this is an act that was planned out or there was forethought before committing the act. The person had time to think about it and consider their actions before committing the act.

Manslaughter is more of an intentional act but not by premediated design. This act in general was not planned.

SCENARIO: Peggy is at work. Her husband Billy is at home. Peggy comes home from work early to Surprise Billy with Dinner. Peggy comes into her home and hears something in her bedroom. She opens the door and sees Billy in bed with another Women having Sex. Peggy starts to scream and reaches into her purse and pulls out her 9mm Pistol and shoots her husband and the girl. They both Die. Peggy had no idea Billy was cheating on her and had no idea of what she was walking into when she went to her bedroom. Can this be Manslaughter? **YES**

SCENARIO: Peggy is at work. Her husband Billy is at home. Peggy comes home from work early to Surprise Billy with Dinner. Peggy comes into her home and hears something in her bedroom. She opens the door and sees Billy in bed with another Women having Sex. Peggy starts to scream and runs out of the Home. She Drives around in her Car for about Ten Minutes thinking about what she saw and the betrayal by her Husband. She then decides that she is going to go back to the home and kill them both. Peggy has a 9mm Pistol she keeps in the Glove Compartment of her car. She gets the gun and loads it inside the vehicle. Peggy drives back to the home and enters the bedroom where Billy and the Girl were getting dressed. Peggy walks up to both and shoots them both in the head killing them. Can this be Murder? **YES**

In the above scenarios you can see that with Manslaughter there was no planning or Forethought. When it came to murder, there was forethought. The shooter left the residence and drove around and after thinking about the situation decided to get a gun load it return to the home and kill two people.

CHAPTER 790
WEAPONS AND FIREARMS

790.01   Unlicensed carrying of concealed weapons or concealed firearms.

(1)   Except as provided in subsection (3), a person who is not licensed under s. 790.06 and who carries a concealed weapon or electric weapon or device on or about his or her person commits a misdemeanor of the first degree, punishable as provided in s. 775.082 or s. 775.083.

(2)   Except as provided in subsection (3), a person who is not licensed under s. 790.06 and who carries a concealed firearm on or about his or her person commits a felony of the third degree, punishable as provided in s. 775.082, s. 775.083, or s. 775.084.

(3)   This section does not apply to:

(a)   A person who carries a concealed weapon, or a person who may lawfully possess a firearm and who carries a concealed firearm, on or about his or her person while in the act of evacuating during a mandatory evacuation order issued during a state of emergency declared by the Governor pursuant to chapter 252 or declared by a local authority pursuant to chapter 870. As used in this subsection, the term "in the act of evacuating" means the immediate and urgent movement of a person away from the evacuation zone within 48 hours after a mandatory evacuation is ordered. The 48 hours may be extended by an order issued by the Governor.

(b)   A person who carries for purposes of lawful self-defense in a concealed manner:

1.   A self-defense chemical spray.

2.   A nonlethal stun gun or dart-firing stun gun or other nonlethal electric weapon or device that is designed solely for defensive purposes.

(4)   This section does not preclude any prosecution for the use of an electric weapon or device, a dart-firing stun gun, or a self-defense chemical spray during the commission of any criminal

(Read Unlicensed Carrying). This Statute reviews the Unlicensed Carrying of Concealed weapons or Firearms. The basics of this Statue is to remember in General if a Person is carrying a gun concealed upon their person or Carrying a Firearm openly without any proper licensing from the Florida Division of Agriculture can be charge with a Felony of the Third Degree. A person can for defensive purposes carry CONCEALED or OPENLY a can of Pepper spray, with no more than 2oz. of Spray, or a stun gun, or Taser with Dart firing cords not to reach further than 15 Feet when deployed.

790.10   Improper exhibition of dangerous weapons or firearms If any person having or carrying any dirk, sword, sword cane, firearm, electric weapon or device, or other weapon shall, in the presence of one or more persons, exhibit the same in a rude, careless, angry, or threatening manner, not in necessary self-defense, the person so offending shall be guilty of a misdemeanor of the first degree, punishable as provided in s. 775.082 or s. 775.083.

(Read Improper Exhibition of Dangerous weapons or firearms). This Statute reviews the instances where a person dangerously displays a weapon or firearm.

SCENARIO: Billy just got a new 9mm Glock Firearm. He went to his friends Bobby's job at the local Grocery Store. Billy takes the gun out of a box in the store and starts to waive it around to show his friend. There are customers in the store that were in fear that the gun could go off and was scared by Billy's waiving around of the gun. Can this be Improper Exhibition?
YES

790.163   False report concerning planting a bomb, an explosive, or a weapon of mass destruction, or concerning the use of firearms in a violent manner/ penalty

(1)   It is unlawful for any person to make a false report, with intent to deceive, mislead, or otherwise misinform any person, concerning the placing or planting of any bomb, dynamite, other deadly explosive, or weapon of mass destruction as defined in s. 790.166, or concerning the use of firearms in a violent manner against a person or persons. A person who violates this subsection commits a felony of the second degree, punishable as provided in s. 775.082, s. 775.083, or s. 775.084.

(Read False Reporting of Bomb). This Statute goes over someone making false reports of planting of bomb or other destructive devices.

SCENARIO: Billy is a Highschool Student. He decides he wishes to get out of going to a certain class. He decides to use his cell phone to call the School and say that there was a Bomb at the School set to go off at 2pm. This causes the School to evacuate and have law

Enforcement do a sweep of the School. Can this be False Report of Planting a Bomb? **YES.** Can Billy Be Charged Criminally**? YES**

790.165 Planting of "hoax bomb" prohibited/ penalties

(1) For the purposes of this section, "hoax bomb" means any device or object that by its design, construction, content, or characteristics appears to be, or to contain, or is represented to be or to contain, a destructive device or explosive as defined in this chapter, but is, in fact, an inoperative facsimile or imitation of such a destructive device or explosive, or contains no destructive device or explosive as was represented.

(2) Any person who, without lawful authority, manufactures, possesses, sells, delivers, sends, mails, displays, uses, threatens to use, attempts to use, or conspires to use, or who makes readily accessible to others, a hoax bomb commits a felony of the second degree, punishable as provided in s. 775.082, s. 775.083, or s. 775.084.

(Read Hoax Bomb). This Statute reviews the actual Planting of a Hoax Bomb.

SCENARIO: Bobby is upset that he lost his job at a Local 7 eleven store. He goes home and grabs some RED Flairs and a small wind up clock from his home. He goes back to the business and tapes the Flairs together with the clock with wires that appear to be attached to the Clock and Red Flairs. A current employee looks at the front window of the business and sees this Device attached to a poll in the Parking Lot. It appears to be an explosive at first sight. The Parking Lot must be Cleared, and the Business is Cleared a local Bomb Team has to come out to remove the Device which turns out to be a Fake Bomb. Can Bobby be Charged with Planting a Hoax Bomb? **YES.**

790.174   Safe storage of firearms required.

(1)   A person who stores or leaves, on a premise under his or her control, a loaded firearm, as defined in s. 790.001, and who knows or reasonably should know that a minor is likely to gain access to the firearm without the lawful permission of the minor's parent or the person having charge of the minor, or without the supervision required by law, shall keep the firearm in a securely locked box or

container or in a location which a reasonable person would believe to be secure or shall secure it with a trigger lock, except when the person is carrying the firearm on his or her body or within such close proximity thereto that he or she can retrieve and use it as easily and quickly as if he or she carried it on his or her body.

(Read Safe Storage of Firearms). This Statute reviews the Safe storage of Firearms. All persons who own firearms needs to make sure that any firearm they own are stored safely away from the reach of any child that could have access to your Home, Business or Vehicle.

790.19   Shooting into or throwing deadly missiles into dwellings, public or private buildings, occupied or not occupied/ vessels, aircraft, buses, railroad cars, streetcars, or other vehicles Whoever, wantonly or maliciously, shoots at, within, or into, or throws any missile or hurls or projects a stone or other hard substance which would produce death or great bodily harm, at, within, or in any public or private building, occupied or unoccupied, or public or private bus or any train, locomotive, railway car, caboose, cable railway car, street railway car, monorail car, or vehicle of any kind which is being used or occupied by any person, or any boat, vessel, ship, or barge lying in or plying the waters of this state, or aircraft flying through the airspace of this state shall be guilty of a felony of the second degree, punishable as provided in s. 775.082, s. 775.083, or s. 775.084.

(Read Shooting into or throwing deadly missile). This Statute reviews instances where an object that can cause any injury, great bodily Harm or Death. This object was thrown at or into a Car, Home, Business, Government Building, Bus, Train Car, etc.

SCENARIO: Billy is upset at the Post Office for losing his mail. Billy drives down to the Post Office grabs several large rocks and throws them through the Front Windows of the Post Office. Can this be Throwing a Deadly Missile into a **Structure**? **YES**

SCENARIO: Billy is Driving his new Camaro past his high school. As he drives by, another student who hates Billy grabs a rock and throws it at Billy while he is driving in the Vehicle. The Large Rock hits Billy's Front Passenger window causing it to shatter. Billy was not physically Injured. Can this Be Throwing a Deadly Missile into a **Conveyance**? **YES**

790.27   Alteration or removal of firearm serial number or possession, sale, or delivery of firearm with serial number altered or removed prohibited/ penalties.

(1)(a)   It is unlawful for any person to knowingly alter or remove the manufacturer's or importer's serial number from a firearm with intent to disguise the true identity thereof.

(b)   Any person violating paragraph (a) is guilty of a felony of the third degree, punishable as provided in s. 775.082, s. 775.083, or s. 775.084.

(2)(a)   It is unlawful for any person to knowingly sell, deliver, or possess any firearm on which the manufacturer's or importer's serial number has been unlawfully altered or removed.

(b)   Any person violating paragraph (a) is guilty of a misdemeanor of the first degree, punishable as provided in s. 775.082 or s. 775.083.

(3)   This section shall not apply to antique firearms.

(Read Alteration or removal of Firearm Serial number). This Statute reviews the issue with altered serial numbers. If a person sands off the serial number of a Firearm they just committed a Crime. If Someone alters the numbers from a Firearm, they Committed a Crime. If someone is in the possession of a Firearm with altered Serial Numbers, they can be charged Criminally. The Officer can also immediately seize the Firearm whether an arrest is made at that time or not.

CHAPTER 794

SEXUAL BATTERY

794.011   Sexual battery.

(1)   As used in this chapter:

(a)   "Consent" means intelligent, knowing, and voluntary consent and does not include coerced submission. "Consent" shall not be deemed or construed to mean the failure by the alleged victim to offer physical resistance to the offender.

(b)   "Mentally defective" means a mental disease or defect which renders a person temporarily or permanently incapable of appraising the nature of his or her conduct.

(c)   "Mentally incapacitated" means temporarily incapable of appraising or controlling a person's own conduct due to the influence of a narcotic, anesthetic, or intoxicating substance administered without his or her consent or due to any other act committed upon that person without his or her consent.

(d) "Offender" means a person accused of a sexual offense in violation of a provision of this chapter.

(e) "Physically helpless" means unconscious, asleep, or for any other reason physically unable to communicate unwillingness to an act.

(f) "Retaliation" includes, but is not limited to, threats of future physical punishment, kidnapping, false imprisonment or forcible confinement, or extortion.

(g) "Serious personal injury" means great bodily harm or pain, permanent disability, or permanent disfigurement.

(h**) "Sexual battery" means oral, anal, or vaginal penetration by, or union with, the sexual organ of another or the anal or vaginal penetration of another by any other object; however, sexual battery does not include an act done for a bona fide medical purpose.**

(i) "Victim" means a person who has been the object of a sexual offense.

(j)   "Physically incapacitated" means bodily impaired or handicapped and substantially limited in ability to resist or flee.

(Read Sexual Battery). This Statute reviews the Crime of Sexual Battery. This is also Called RAPE. Rape is a term that is used in general public speech, but it is **not** an acceptable term for Florida Criminal Statue. In this Statue read Sections **(a)** and **(h)** very closely. The understanding of this statue is very important when brining charges against an induvial or individuals for a Violation of this Chapter.

SCENARIO: Leroy and Joseph are high school students. They are both 17 years old. They see a disabled 17-year-old girl from there school in a wheelchair waiting for the bus to pick her up at the front of the school. The teacher who was waiting with her walked off back into the school to retrieve something. The girl is disabled to where she cannot walk and has the mentality of a 5-year-old. Both boys see the Teacher walk off and go make contact with the Girl they push her behind the school and take off her clothes. She is not resisting and does not know what they are doing. Both boys pull the girl to the ground and both take turns having sexual intercourse with her. Can both be Charged with

Sexual Battery? YES. They took advantage of a physically and mentally challenge person.

SCENARIO: Leroy is at a party. Leroy sees a girl and decides he was going to have sex with her one-way or the other. He approaches her and starts a conversation. He then starts to feed her drink after drink after drink of alcohol. He sees that she is severely intoxicated and can barely walk. He decides to start to kiss her and she pulls away at first, but she is so intoxicated she falls onto the couch at the party and passes out. Leroy decides to take off her pants and have sexual intercourse with her. She is passed out during the encounter. Can Leroy be Charged with **Sexual Battery**? **YES.**

SCENARIO: Leroy and Sally are on a first date. Leroy picks up sally at her home and they go and have a nice dinner. After dinner they decide to go and have some drinks at a local bar. Leroy and Sally both have been drinking. They both Leave the bar together and Sally invites Leroy up to her apartment for some coffee. They are both sitting on her couch and start kissing. Sally thinks things are going too far and tells Leroy to **STOP**. Leroy persists with trying to take off Sally's Pants. She pushes his hands away from her and tells him, "NO and

STOP" and to leave. Leroy pushes Sally down and forces himself on her. Leroy forces intercourse with Sally. Can Leroy be charged with Sexual Battery? **YES.** When Sally told Leroy to **stop.** He should have **stopped. STOP DOES MEAN STOP! NO MEANS NO!.**

One thing that will be an issue when determining if a crime like Sexual battery had occurred is the "" he said she said", or Date Rape. This is when an Adult person comes to your agency or calls for assistance and tells you that they were Raped. The reportee might have no injuries and no visible signs of being physically forced Or attacked. You then see the alleged Adult offender who states that it was voluntary and that the **reportee** is lying. You as the Law Enforcement Officer will need to judge what you are being told. When it comes to, he said she said you need to tread carefully when deciding what action, you will be immediately taking. Treat your alleged victim as a victim and make sure you take the steps outlined by Departmental policy in handling a Sexual Battery investigation. Including getting the Victim medical treatment to make sure they are ok, and to further gathering evidence for your case. If the alleged perpetrator is there and is providing you with all their information, i.e. Identification, work numbers, address, phone numbers. I might be hesitant to immediately arrest this person. The reason for this is that this person voluntarily stated that a sexual act occurred, BUT that it was mutual and voluntary. Second, this person is giving you all their information which can be used for a Charging affidavit and an address where they live and work in case you need to contact them further, or your Detective or Investigative Division can follow up. The biggest thing to consider in this type of situation is **TIME.** What I mean by this is, the State of Florida allows only a certain amount of days to bring a person to trial after they had been arrested or they can walk free.

So, if you are at a residence and the suspect is there and you make an immediate arrest, the Clock Starts at the time you took this persons Freedom away. Let's say you handcuff this individual and place them in your car to go to the station. You get the suspect there and after further speaking with them you decide to let them go at that time while further investigation is needed by you and your agency. What you have just done now was start a clock that is now continually running.

In Florida, Rule 3.191 "The right to a speedy trial" Trial without Demand by Arrestee, If a Misdemeanor 90 Days, if a Felony 175 Days. Speedy Trial Upon Demand by Arrestee, 60 Days to do formal Indictment or Information being filed.

So, if you "arrest" that individual the clock starts. Most cases like the one we are discussing takes time to collect evidence and you do not want the State Attorney being forced to rush a case. Evidence needs time to be collected and processed. Interviewing of further witnesses might be needed etc.

794.02 Common-law presumption relating to age abolished the common-law rule "that a boy under 14 years of age is conclusively presumed to be incapable of committing the crime of rape" shall not be in force in this state.

(Read Common Law presumption abolished). This Statute reviews that the common law rule "that a boy under the age of 14 is presumed to be incapable of committing Sexual battery", is

not accepted in the State of Florida. A child can be charged with Sexual Battery of another.

794.021   Ignorance or belief as to victim's age no Defense When, in this chapter, the criminality of conduct depends upon the victim's being below a certain specified age, ignorance of the age is no defense. Neither shall misrepresentation of age by such person nor a bona fide belief that such person is over the specified age be a defense.

(Read Ignorance as to victims age). This Statute reviews that any Individual either Male or Female needs to make sure that any person they are sexually involved with or are about to engage in a sexual act is of proper legal age as outlined by Florida State Statue. Simply Stating" I didn't know", will not avoid that person from being charged Criminally.

794.027   Duty to report sexual battery/ penalties   A person who observes the commission of the crime of sexual battery and who:

(1)   Has reasonable grounds to believe that he or she has observed the commission of a sexual battery/

(2)   Has the present ability to seek assistance for the victim or victims by immediately reporting such offense to a law enforcement officer/

(3)   Fails to seek such assistance;

(4)   Would not be exposed to any threat of physical violence for seeking such assistance;

(5)   Is not the husband, wife, parent, grandparent, child, grandchild, brother, or sister of the offender or victim, by consanguinity or affinity/ and

(6)   Is not the victim of such sexual battery

(Read Duty to report Sexual Battery). This Statute reviews the duties of a person should they have knowledge that a Sexual Battery. Now this statue covers if they OBSERVED an incident. That they need to make a report of this immediately to Law Enforcement.

Now I want to bring something else to this statue, there was a Law Enforcement Officer in the Florida County where I had worked, who had knowledge that a Sexual battery that had occurred to an Adult Female. He was not on Duty at the time, BUT the female victim confided in him to make a report of what had occurred to her. He advised his agency that he knew about the Sexual battery complaint by the Female, and it occurred in a different Jurisdiction in the Same County, so he did not feel he needed to report it, BUT that he was off duty and not Superman.

Mr. "Not Superman" was also Mr. "Unemployed" after an Internal Investigation into his conduct.

794.05 Unlawful sexual activity with certain minors

(1) A person 24 years of age or older who engages in sexual activity with a person 16 or 17 years of age commits a felony of the second degree, punishable as provided in s. 775.082, s. 775.083, or s. 775.084. As used in this section, "sexual activity" means oral, anal, or vaginal penetration by, or union with, the sexual organ of another or the anal or vaginal penetration of another by any other object, however, sexual

activity does not include an act done for a bona fide medical purpose.

(2)   The provisions of this section do not apply to a person 16 or 17 years of age who has had the disabilities of nonage removed under chapter 743.

(3)   The victim's prior sexual conduct is not a relevant issue in a prosecution under this section.

(4)   If an offense under this section directly results in the victim giving birth to a child, paternity of that child shall be established as described in chapter 742. If it is determined that the offender is the father of the child, the offender must pay child support pursuant to the child support guidelines described in chapter 61.

(Read Unlawful Sexual Activity with Certain Minors). This Statute reviews unlawful sexual activities with CERTAIN minors. The provision in this statue has changed over time. At one time, anyone having a sexual relationship or encounter with a person under 18 years age had committed a Crime. I cannot speak for the Florida Legislatures that had made changes to this statue, but at one time if a girl of 17 was dating her boyfriend who was 18 and having a sexual relationship that Boyfriend could have been arrested for Sexual Battery. Which also destroyed the boy's life especially if both were later married or the girl became pregnant and there was no support for the child since the 18-year-old was now serving time.

So, there is something of a VOID in respect to age and consent. Read this statue very carefully. If a person is 21 years old and is dating a 17-year-old there is **nothing** there to charge the 21-year-old with. It's like a voided space.

You will also deal with issues like let's say two 15-year-old's Boy and Girl have a sexual relationship. They are both minors and under 16 years of age. This is something that I had to deal with. I had a parent come to the Police Department saying his daughter was Raped by a Boy her age from School. Contact was made with the boys' parents and I had both at my Agency. It was determined that they were Boyfriend and Girlfriend. No one was forced and they both told me that they loved each other. The father of the girl was right and told me his daughter could not give consent and was considered a child and he wanted that boy arrested. I advised that parent that I could charge the boy, but that his daughter could also be charged with the same Crime. That the boy would also be a victim from his daughter. Both parents spoke with each other. I advised both parents that Children at times will experiment with sex. That in leu of Criminal Charges that there may be other ways of handling this situation, but that I would leave it up to them to decide which way this was going to go. After a short period of time both parents agreed that this was more of a Family issue and they would rather pursue alternative resources privately like Family Counseling or therapy. I did not charge anyone with anything.

Good Common Sense and Judgment is essential in Law Enforcement. The actions that I took in this situation might not be the actions you would have taken. But before I would destroy a child's life with a serious charge of Sexual Battery, I would have to look at exactly what had occurred. Law Enforcement is not only done from a Statue book, but also from the heart, and with Good Judgement, Good Common Sense and Good Decision-Making Abilities.

CHAPTER 800

LEWDNESS/ INDECENT EXPOSURE

800.03   Exposure of sexual organs It is unlawful to expose or exhibit one's sexual organs in public or on the private premises of another, or so near thereto as to be seen from such private premises, in a vulgar or indecent manner, or to be naked in public except in any place provided or set apart for that purpose. Violation of this section is a misdemeanor of the first degree, punishable as provided in s. 775.082 or s. 775.083. A mother's breastfeeding of her baby does not under any circumstance violate this section.

(Read Lewdness; Indecent Exposure). This Statute reviews the Exposure of Sexual Organs. In discussing this topic, you need to understand something very clearly **A WOMEN CANNOT EXPOSE THEIR SEXUAL ORGANS.** Only a **MAN** can Expose themselves. A women's sexual organs are inside their body. A man's sexual organs are outside their bodies. A women's "breast" is **not** considered a Sexual Organ.

SCENARIO: Billy is 16 years old and his Friends dare him to expose himself to a group of ladies sitting at a local Park. Billy thinks he is funny and pulls his pants down flashing his genitals at the ladies and takes off and runs. Can Billy be charged with Exposure of a Sexual Organ? **YES**

SCENARIO: Billy's Dad Howard has been drinking a lot and is drunk. He takes off his clothes and pulls open the blinds to his home and starts dancing naked Infront of the window for all the neighbors to see. People are walking by are stopping to watch Howard Dance. Can Howard be charged with Indecent Exposure**?** **YES.** For this one Howard can dance Naked in his house all he wants, but once he pulled open all the blinds so people can see him then the Crime was committed.

CHAPTER 806

ARSON AND CRIMINAL MISCHIEF

806.101   False alarms of fires Whoever, without reasonable cause, by outcry or the ringing of bells, or otherwise, makes or circulates, or causes to be made or circulated, a false alarm of fire, shall for the first conviction be guilty of a misdemeanor of the first degree, punishable as provided in s. 775.082 or s. 775.083. A second or subsequent conviction under this section shall constitute a felony of the third degree, punishable as provided in s. 775.082, s. 775.083, or s. 775.084.

(Read False alarms of Fires). This Statute reviews individuals Falsely Reporting fires. This occurs in different ways, one way you would be dealing with as a Law Enforcement Officer is when someone pulls a Fire alarm Station in a Building, a School an Apartment Complex or other location that has pull Station. They do this intentionally to cause a disturbance or Panic. There is no Fire.

806.13   Criminal mischief/penalties/penalty for minor

(1)(a)   A person commits the offense of criminal mischief if he or she willfully and maliciously injures or damages by any means any real or personal property belonging to another, including, but not limited to, the placement of graffiti thereon or other acts of vandalism thereto.

(b)1.   If the damage to such property is $200 or less, it is a misdemeanor of the second degree, punishable as provided in s. 775.082 or s. 775.083.

2.   If the damage to such property is greater than $200 but less than $1,000, it is a misdemeanor of the first degree, punishable as provided in s. 775.082 or s. 775.083.

3.   If the damage is $1,000 or greater, or if there is interruption or impairment of a business operation or public communication, transportation, supply of water, gas or power, or other public service which costs $1,000 or more in labor and supplies to restore, it is a

felony of the third degree, punishable as provided in s. 775.082, s. 775.083, or s. 775.084.

4.   If the person has one or more previous convictions for violating this subsection, the offense under subparagraph 1. or subparagraph 2. for which the person is charged shall be reclassified as a felony of the third degree, punishable as provided in s. 775.082, s. 775.083, or s. 775.084.

(2)   Any person who willfully and maliciously defaces, injures, or damages by any means any church, synagogue, mosque, or other place of worship, or any religious article contained therein, commits a felony of the third degree, punishable as provided in s. 775.082, s. 775.083, or s. 775.084, if the damage to the property is greater than $200.

(3)   Whoever, without the consent of the owner thereof, willfully destroys or substantially damages any public telephone, or telephone cables, wires, fixtures, antennas, amplifiers, or any other apparatus, equipment, or appliances, which destruction or damage renders a public telephone inoperative or which

opens the body of a public telephone, commits a felony of the third degree, punishable as provided in s. 775.082, s. 775.083, or s. 775.084/ provided, however, that a conspicuous notice of the provisions of this subsection and the penalties provided is posted on or near the destroyed or damaged instrument and visible to the public at the time of the commission of the offense.

(Read Criminal Mischief). This Statute reviews Acts of Criminal Mischief committed by individuals. This is the act of Damaging others property for malicious purposes.

SCENARIO: Billy hates his next-door neighbors. At 2am in the morning he sneaks over to the neighbor's home. They have a Black Camaro parked in the driveway. Billy takes a screwdriver and scratches up the left side of the vehicle causing damaged to the drivers outside drivers' door. Can Billy be charged with Criminal Mischief? YES.

SCENARIO: Billy and his friend Steve hate there Highschool. They both go to the school at 3am and Spray Paint Graffiti over all the front windows and doors of the school. Can they be charged with Criminal Mischief? **YES**

CHAPTER 810
BURGLARY AND TRESPASS

(1) "Structure" means a building of any kind, either temporary or permanent, which has a roof over it, together with the curtilage thereof. However, during the time of a state of emergency declared by executive order or proclamation of the Governor under chapter 252 and within the area covered by such executive order or proclamation and for purposes of ss. 810.02 and 810.08 only, the term means a building of any kind or such portions or remnants thereof as exist at the original site, regardless of absence of a wall or roof.

(2) "Dwelling" means a building or conveyance of any kind, including any attached porch, whether such building or conveyance is temporary or permanent, mobile or immobile, which has a roof over it and is designed to be occupied by people lodging therein at night, together with the curtilage thereof. However,

during the time of a state of emergency declared by executive order or proclamation of the Governor under chapter 252 and within the area covered by such executive order or proclamation and for purposes of ss. 810.02 and 810.08 only, the term includes such portions or remnants thereof as exist at the original site, regardless of absence of a wall or roof.

(3) "Conveyance" means any motor vehicle, ship, vessel, railroad vehicle or car, trailer, aircraft, or sleeping car, and "to enter a conveyance" includes taking apart any portion of the conveyance. However, during the time of a state of emergency declared by executive order or proclamation of the Governor under chapter 252 and within the area covered by such executive order or proclamation and for purposes of ss. 810.02 and 810.08 only, the term "conveyance" means a motor vehicle, ship, vessel, railroad vehicle or car, trailer, aircraft, or sleeping car or such portions thereof as exist.

(Read Structure, Dwelling and Conveyance). An easy way to remember these definitions is this; A STRUCTURE anything with Four Walls and a Roof. A Back yard Shed, Business Building, Office Building, Barn, etc. DWELLING, a House, Apartment, Motel, Hotel, anything built for a person to sleep in overnight. CONVEYANCE, a Car, Boat, Truck, Train, Plane.

810.02 Burglary

(1)(a)   For offenses committed on or before July 1, 2001, "burglary" means entering or remaining in a dwelling, a structure, or a conveyance with the intent to commit an offense therein, unless the premises are at the time open to the public or the defendant is licensed or invited to enter or remain.

(b)   For offenses committed after July 1, 2001, "burglary" means:

1.   Entering a dwelling, a structure, or a conveyance with the intent to commit an offense therein, unless the premises are at the time open to the public or the defendant is licensed or invited to enter; or

2.   Notwithstanding a licensed or invited entry, remaining in a dwelling, structure, or conveyance:

a.   Surreptitiously, with the intent to commit an offense therein;

b.   After permission to remain therein has been withdrawn, with the intent to commit an offense therein.

(Read Burglary). This Statute reviews the Offense of Burglary. Read this carefully. Remember burglary is to enter a Conveyance, Dwelling or a Structure to commit a Crime therein. Now understand that is says a **Crime therein**.

This means <u>ANY CRIME</u>. If someone smashes the window of your car enters the car and steals the stereo that would be Burglary. If someone walks up to your car at a traffic light and reaches into your car Window and punches you on the nose, that would be Burglary also. Someone breaks into your home while you are on vacation, nothing was stolen but they spray painted your living room, that would also be Burglary.   Burglary statue will always precede with another Statue, like Burglary Battery for the punch on the nose. Burglary Petit theft if the Radio stolen from the vehicle was valued under $750.00 dollars. Burglary Criminal Mischief for the spray painting inside your home when you went away.

Remember it's not only stealing from, but any crime committed therein.

810.08   Trespass in structure or conveyance

(1)   Whoever, without being authorized, licensed, or invited, willfully enters **or** remains in any structure **or** conveyance, **or**, having been authorized, licensed, or invited, is warned by the owner **or** lessee of the premises, **or** by a person authorized by the owner **or** lessee, to depart and refuses to do so, commits the offense of trespass in a structure or conveyance.

(2)(a)   Except as otherwise provided in this subsection, trespass in a structure or conveyance is a misdemeanor of the second degree, punishable as provided in s. 775.082 or s. 775.083.

(b)   If there is a human being in the structure or conveyance at the time the offender trespassed, attempted to trespass, or was in the structure or conveyance, the trespass in a structure or conveyance is a misdemeanor of the first degree, punishable as provided in s. 775.082 or s. 775.083.

(c)   If the offender is armed with a firearm or other dangerous weapon, or arms himself or herself with such while in the structure or conveyance, the trespass in a structure or conveyance is a felony of the third degree, punishable as provided in s. 775.082, s. 775.083, or s. 775.084. Any owner or person authorized by the owner may, for prosecution purposes, take into custody and detain, in a reasonable manner, for a reasonable length of time, any person when he or she reasonably believes that a violation of this paragraph has been or is being committed, and he or she reasonably believes that the person to be taken into custody and detained has committed or is committing such violation. In the event a person is taken into custody, a law enforcement officer shall be called as soon as is practicable after the person has been taken into custody. The taking into custody and detention by such person, if done in compliance with the requirements of this paragraph, shall not render such person criminally or civilly liable for false arrest, false imprisonment, or unlawful detention.

(3)   As used in this section, the term "person authorized" means any owner or lessee, or his or her agent, or any law enforcement officer whose department has received written authorization from the owner or lessee, or his or her agent, to communicate an order to depart the property in the case of a threat to public safety or welfare.

Read (Trespass in Structure or Conveyance). This Statute reviews the instances when an individual trespass in a Structure or Conveyance.

SCENARIO: Billy is Homeless and decides he wants to get out of the cold. Billy walks by a Black BMW and the driver's door appears to be unsecured. Billy pulls and forces the door open. He then climbs inside the car. He doesn't steal anything, and he doesn't damage anything inside the car. Can Billy be Charged with Trespassing in a Conveyance? **YES**

SCENARIO: Billy's Father owns a small hardware store downtown. A customer in the store starts to yell at Billy's Father. Billy's Father tells this customer several times to just

leave the store. The customer refuses. Can this
Customer be Charged with Trespassing? YES

810.09   Trespass on property other than structure or conveyance

(1)(a)   A person who, without being authorized, licensed, or invited, willfully enters upon or remains in any property other than a structure or conveyance:

1.   As to which notice against entering or remaining is given, either by actual communication to the offender or by posting, fencing, or cultivation as described in s. 810.011; or

2.   If the property is the unenclosed curtilage of a dwelling and the offender enters or remains with the intent to commit an offense thereon, other than the offense of trespass,

Read (Trespass on property other than a structure or conveyance). This Statute reviews the Offense of Trespass. In this instant this would be trespass in a Home, Residence, Land, Curtilage around a property.

SCENARIO: Billy and his Friend Steve decide to take a short cut home from school. They decide to walk through their Neighbors property. They have no permission to enter his property. Could they be charged with Trespassing? **YES**

SCENARIO: Officer Bob is dispatched to a Hotel where it was reported that there was an unknown person in one of the rooms. Officer Bob goes to the room and finds an adult male with a backpack staying in the room. Through his investigation he discovers this person had snuck onto the property and found an open room. Can this adult male be charged with Trespassing in property other than a structure or Conveyance? **YES**

810.14   Voyeurism prohibited/ penalties

(1)   A person commits the offense of voyeurism when he or she, with lewd, lascivious, or indecent intent:

(a)   Secretly observes another person when the other person is in a dwelling, structure, or conveyance and such location provides a reasonable expectation of privacy.

(b)   Secretly observes another person's intimate areas in which the person has a reasonable expectation of privacy, when the other person is in a public or private dwelling, structure, or conveyance. As used in this paragraph, the term "intimate area" means any portion of a person's body or undergarments that is covered by clothing and intended to be protected from public view.

(2)   A person who violates this section commits a misdemeanor of the first degree for the first violation, punishable as provided in s. 775.082 or s. 775.083.

(3)   A person who violates this section and who has been previously convicted or adjudicated delinquent two or more times of any violation of this section commits a felony of the third degree, punishable as provided in s. 775.082, s. 775.083, or s. 775.084.

(4)   For purposes of this section, a person has been previously convicted or adjudicated delinquent of a violation of this section if the violation resulted in a conviction sentenced separately, or an adjudication of delinquency entered separately, prior to the current offense.

Read (Voyeurism). This Statute reviews the Offense of Voyeurism.

SCENARIO: Billy likes his neighbors Mom next to his house. He decides one night to sneak over to the Neighbors house. He sneaks up to the Bathroom window while his neighbors MOM is in the Shower. Billy gets Caught by His Friends Father. Can Billy be charge with Voyeurism? YES.

SCENARIO: Officer Bob is shopping with his 19-year-old Daughter. His daughter decides to go and try on some new pants. When she goes into the changing room, she sees a little mirror in the top corner of the room reflecting down to the next, changing room. She calls out to her father who comes in and catches Billy the stock boy with mirrors and camera equipment. Billy was using the mirrors to watch people undressing and was photographing the images. Can Billy the stock boy be charged with Voyeurism? **YES.**

CHAPTER 812

THEFT, ROBBERY, AND RELATED CRIMES

812.014   Theft

(1)   A person commits theft if he or she knowingly obtains or uses, or endeavors to obtain or to use, the property of another with intent to, either temporarily or permanently:

(a)   Deprive the other person of a right to the property or a benefit from the property.

(b)   Appropriate the property to his or her own use or to the use of any person not entitled to the use of the property.

Read (THEFT). This Statute reviews the Offense Theft.

If the item(s) taken from an Individual is used by another with the intent to either temporarily or permanently deprive that individual, then a crime has occurred.

If an item or some property taken is valued at less than **$750** Dollars in Value, it is a **Misdemeanor.** If an item or property taken is valued at **$750** Dollars or Greater, then that would be a **Felony.**

SCENARIO: Billy goes to a clothing store and decides he is going to steal some clothes. Billy is stopped by a store employee and Officer Bob responds to the Store. When the store employee added up all the clothes that Billy left the store with it came out to **$749.99**. Can Billy be Charge with **Misdemeanor Petit Theft**? **YES.** Billy can be charged with this because the total value of items stolen are less than $**750.00 Dollars.**

SCENARIO: Billy goes to a clothing store and decides he is going to steal some clothes. Billy is stopped by a store employee and Officer Bob responds to the Store. When the store employee added up all the clothes that Billy left the store with it came out to **$750.00**. Can Billy be Charge with **Felony Grand Theft? YES.** This is since the value of the items stolen is valued at **$750.00** Dollars or higher.

812.13 Robbery

(1) "Robbery" means the taking of money or other property which may be the subject of larceny from the person or custody of another, with intent to either permanently or temporarily deprive the person or the owner of the money or other property, when in the course of the taking there is the use of force, violence, assault, or putting in fear.

(2)(a) If in the course of committing the robbery the offender carried a firearm or other deadly weapon, then the robbery is a felony of the first degree, punishable by imprisonment for a term of years not exceeding life imprisonment or as provided in s. 775.082, s. 775.083, or s. 775.084.

(b) If in the course of committing the robbery the offender carried a weapon, then the robbery is a felony of the first degree, punishable as provided in s. 775.082, s. 775.083, or s. 775.084.

(c) If in the course of committing the robbery the offender carried no firearm, deadly weapon, or other weapon, then the robbery is a felony of the second degree, punishable as provided in s. 775.082, s. 775.083, or s. 775.084.

(3)(a) An act shall be deemed "in the course of committing the robbery" if it occurs in an attempt to commit robbery or in flight after the attempt or commission.

(b) An act shall be deemed "in the course of the taking" if it occurs either prior to, contemporaneous with, or subsequent to the taking of the property and if it and the act of taking constitute a continuous series of acts or events.

Read (Robbery). This Statute reviews the Offense of Robbery. It is important to remember that Robbery is always from a **PERSON.** You **cannot** Rob a **Business,** but you can rob the people therein

SCENARIO: Billy needs money and comes up with an Idea that when he sees someone by an ATM, he will sneak up to them and Rob them for their Money. Billy does not have a gun. Billy sees an elderly man getting money from an ATM. Billy walks up to the elderly man and states "Give me your Money and Watch or I am going to Punch your Face In" Billy is 24 years old '60 Tall 210 lbs. The elderly man is terrified and gives Billy his money and Watch. Can Billy be charged with Robbery? **YES.** But what kind of Robbery? **STRONG ARMED ROBBERY**

It is strong armed robbery because Billy did not use a weapon or Gun. He did make threats to the victim, which put fear into the victim compelling him to give Billy what he wanted.

SCENARIO: Billy is walking down the street wearing his new 14k gold neckless. Johnny sees Billy wearing this neckless and follows Billy down the Block. Billy does not know Johnny. Johnny walk's up to Billy Grabbing him around his throat and slamming Billy to the Ground. Johnny kicks Billy several times and then reaches down and rips the Gold Necklace off Billy's Neck. Johnny then runs away. Can Johnny be charged with Strong Armed Robbery? **YES.** Johnny used physical force to attack Billy and steal his Neckless off him.

SCENARIO: Billy is a Meth Head and needs money. Billy gets a gun from one of his friends and stakes at a Bank ATM. Billy sees a young girl using the ATM. As she turns to walk away from the ATM Billy Jumps at her pointing his 38cal. Revolver in her face. He demands her to give him her money or he was going to shoot her. She is terrified and gives Billy her purse. Billy takes off running. Can Billy be Charged with ARMED ROBBERY? **YES.** Billy used a Firearm to Rob the Female.

SCENARIO: Billy needs money badly. Billy thinks of how he could get some money fast. He comes up with an idea to Rob a Bank. He has no gun or weapon, so he decides to put his hand inside his coat pocket and pretend that he has a gun. Billy goes into the Bank and walks to a teller. He demands money from the teller pointing his hand in his jacket at the teller, telling the teller that he had a Gun and he would shoot if the teller didn't fill his bag with Money. The teller is terrified and sees what appears to them to be a gun hidden in Billy's

Jacket pointing at them. The teller fills the bag and Billy Runs out. 2o minutes Later Billy is Caught several Blocks away. He tells the Police Officers that he did do the crime but did **not** have a gun, that he was faking it. The Police did not find a Gun on Billy when he was Caught. Can Billy be Charged with ARMED ROBBERY? **YES.**
Billy implied that he had a gun putting the tellers in fear that they were going to be shot. So, yes, he can be charged with Armed Robbery.

812.131   Robbery by sudden snatching

(1)   "Robbery by sudden snatching", means the taking of money or other property from the victim's person, with intent to permanently or temporarily deprive the victim or the owner of the money or other property, when, in the course of the taking, the victim was or became aware of the taking. In order to satisfy this definition, it is not necessary to show that:

(a)   The offender used any amount of force beyond that effort necessary to obtain possession of the money or other property; or

(b)   There was any resistance offered by the victim to the offender or that there was injury to the victim's person.

(2)(a)   If, in the course of committing a robbery by sudden snatching, the offender carried a firearm or other deadly weapon, the robbery by sudden snatching is a felony of the second degree, punishable as provided in s. 775.082, s. 775.083, or s. 775.084.

(b)   If, in the course of committing a robbery by sudden snatching, the offender carried no firearm or other deadly weapon, the robbery by sudden snatching is a felony of the third degree, punishable as provided in s. 775.082, s. 775.083, or s. 775.084.

(3)(a)   An act shall be deemed "in the course of committing a robbery by sudden snatching" if the act occurs in an attempt to commit robbery by sudden snatching or in fleeing after the attempt or commission.

(b)   An act shall be deemed "in the course of the taking" if the act occurs prior to, contemporaneous with, or subsequent to the taking of the property and if such act and the act of taking constitute a continuous series of acts or events.

Read (Robbery by sudden snatching). This Statute reviews the Offense of Robbery. It is important to remember that Robbery is always from a **PERSON.** You **cannot** Rob a **Business,** but you can rob the people therein.

SCENARIO: Mary and her daughter go shopping. As Mary and her daughter are walking through the Shopping Lot Parking lot, Billy comes running through the lot and grabs for the purse over Mary's shoulder. Mary holds onto the purse and Billy pulls the purse snatching from her hands. Billy then runs off. Can this be Robbery by Sudden Snatching? YES. It can also be Strong Armed Robbery.

SCENARIO: Mary and her daughter go shopping. As Mary and her daughter are walking through the Shopping Lot Parking lot, Billy comes slowly through the lot and uses a pair of scissors to cut the purse strap off Mary. Mary realizes that her purse appeared to come off her shoulder and turns and sees Billy with her purse running.   Can this be Robbery by Sudden Snatching? **YES.** Billy did not use force to take the purse from Mary, BUT he did get her purse and she became aware of what he was doing.

CHAPTER 831
FORGERY AND COUNTERFEITING

831.01   Forgery Whoever falsely makes, alters, forges or counterfeits a public record, or a certificate, return or attestation of any clerk or register of a court, public register, notary public, town clerk or any public officer, in relation to a matter wherein such certificate, return or attestation may be received as a legal proof; or a charter, deed, will, testament, bond, or writing obligatory, letter of attorney, policy of insurance, bill of lading, bill of exchange or promissory note, or an order, acquittance, or discharge for money or other property, or an acceptance of a bill of exchange or promissory note for the payment of money, or any receipt for money, goods or other property, or any passage ticket, pass or other evidence of transportation issued by a common carrier, with intent to injure or defraud any person, shall be guilty of a felony of the third degree, punishable as provided in s. 775.082, s. 775.083, or s. 775.084.

Read (Forgery). This Statute reviews the Offense of Forgery.

SCENARIO: Billy is living with his Father. Billy is 22 years old and does not work. He sees that his Dad, leaves his Bank Book on their Kitchen Table. He takes a check from the Bank Book with the intent to steal money from his Fathers account. Billy fills the Check out for $150.00 Dollars. He writes the check out to himself Billy Smith. Billy then signed his Father's Name Charlie Smith to the check as an Endorsement. Can this be Forgery of his Fathers Signature? **YES**

831.02   Uttering forged instruments

Whoever utters and publishes as true a false, forged or altered record, deed, instrument or other writing mentioned in s. 831.01 knowing the same to be false, altered, forged or counterfeited, with intent to injure or defraud any person, shall be guilty of a felony of the third degree, punishable as provided in s. 775.082, s. 775.083, or s. 775.084.

Read (Uttering a Forged Instrument). This Statute reviews the Offense of Forgery.

SCENARIO: Billy is living with his Father. Billy is 22 years old and does not work. He sees that his Dad, leaves his Bank Book on their Kitchen Table. He takes a check from the Bank Book with the intent to steal money from his Fathers account. Billy fills the Check out for $150.00 Dollars. He writes the check out to himself Billy Smith. Billy then signed his Father's Name Charlie Smith to the check as an Endorsement. He then takes the check and gives it to the teller to cash it. Can this be Uttering a Forged Instrument? YES. Once Billy gave it to the teller it was now Uttered.

CHAPTER 837

PERJURY

837.05   False reports to law enforcement authorities

(1)(a)   Except as provided in paragraph (b) or subsection (2), a person who knowingly gives false information to a law enforcement officer concerning the alleged commission of any crime, commits a misdemeanor of the first degree, punishable as provided in s. 775.082 or s. 775.083.

(b)   A person who commits a violation of paragraph (a) commits a felony of the third degree, punishable as provided in s. 775.082, s. 775.083, or s. 775.084, if the person has previously been convicted of a violation of paragraph (a) and subparagraph 1. or subparagraph 2. applies:

1.   The information the person gave to the law enforcement officer was communicated orally and the officer's account of that information is corroborated by:

a.   An audio recording or audio recording in a video of that information;

b.   A written, or recorded statement made by the person who gave that information, or

c.   Another person who was present when that person gave that information to the officer and heard that information.

2.   The information the person gave to the law enforcement officer was communicated in writing.

(2)   A person who knowingly gives false information to a law enforcement officer concerning the alleged commission of a capital felony, commits a felony of the third degree, punishable as provided in s. 775.082, s. 775.083, or s. 775.084.

Read (False reports to a Law Enforcement). This Statute reviews the Offense of Reporting False Crimes to Law Enforcement.

SCENARIO: Billy has a Beautiful new Ford Mustang. He and His girlfriend Peggy are at a Local Bar Drinking. Peggy gets very intoxicated and tells Billy, that she wanted to drive his car. Billy gives her the keys. She and her girlfriend walk outside of the Bar and takes Billy car for a Joy Ride. Two miles down the road Peggy collides with another vehicle. She and her

Friend run from the crash leaving Billy's Car at the scene of the Crash. Peggy gets scared and calls Billy and tells him what she had done. Billy tells her to go home and he calls the Police and reports that his Car was **stolen earlier,** and he does not know who could have taken it. Can Billy be charged with False Report to a Law Enforcement Officer? **YES**

CHAPTER 843
OBSTRUCTING JUSTICE

843.01   Resisting officer with violence to his or her person Whoever knowingly and willfully resists, obstructs, or opposes any officer as defined in s. 943.10(1), (2), (3), (6), (7), (8), or (9); member of the Florida Commission on Offender Review or any administrative aide or supervisor employed by the commission; parole and probation supervisor; county probation officer; personnel or representative of the Department of Law Enforcement; or other person legally authorized to execute process in the execution of legal process or in the lawful execution of any legal duty, by offering or doing violence to the person of such officer or legally authorized person, is guilty of a felony of the third degree, punishable as provided in s. 775.082, s. 775.083, or s. 775.084.

Read (Resisting Officer with Violence). This Statute reviews the Offense of Resisting Officer **with Violence**).

125

SCENARIO: Billy had a warrant for his arrest for Petit Theft. Officer Bob sees Billy walking down the street. Officer Bob checked his computer and saw that the warrant was active for Billy's arrest. He stops Billy and informs him that there was a warrant for his arrest. He tells Billy to turn around so he can handcuff him. Billy turns around and then Kicks Officer Bob in the Stomach and runs. Can Billy be Charged with Resisting Arrest with Violence? **YES**

843.02   Resisting officer without violence to his or her person Whoever shall resist, obstruct, or oppose any officer as defined in s. 943.10(1), (2), (3), (6), (7), (8), or (9); member of the Florida Commission on Offender Review or any administrative aide or supervisor employed by the commission; county probation officer, parole and probation supervisor, personnel or representative of the Department of Law Enforcement, or other person legally authorized to execute process in the execution of legal process or in the lawful execution of any legal duty, without offering or doing violence to the person of the officer, shall be guilty of a misdemeanor of the first degree, punishable as provided in s. 775.082 or s. 775.083.

Read (Resisting Officer **without** Violence). This Statute reviews the Offense of Resisting Officer **without Violence**).

SCENARIO: Billy had a warrant for his arrest for Petit Theft. Officer Bob sees Billy walking down the street. Officer Bob checked his computer and saw that the warrant was active for Billy's arrest. He stops Billy and informs him that

127

there was a warrant for his arrest. He tells Billy to turn around so he can handcuff him. Billy turns around and then turns back around and tells Officer Bob that he is not going to Jail. Officer Bob has to then reach out and grab Billy and place his hands behind his back. AS Officer Bob tries to place the Handcuffs on Billy. Billy tightens up his arms to resist Officer Bob from placing the handcuffs on. Billy never struck or hit Officer Bob. Can Billy be charged with Resisting arrest without Violence? **YES.** In this scenario this would **not be** resisting with Violence, because Billy's resistance was Active but **not** violent to Officer Bob.

843.03   Obstruction by disguised person

Whoever in any manner disguises himself or herself with intent to obstruct the due execution of the law, or with the intent to intimidate, hinder, or interrupt any officer, beverage enforcement agent, or other person in the legal performance of his or her duty or the exercise of his or her rights under the constitution or laws of this state, whether such intent is effected or not, shall be guilty of a misdemeanor of the first degree, punishable as provided in s. 775.082 or s. 775.083.

Read (Resisting Officer with Violence). This Statute reviews the Offense of Resisting Officer with Violence).

SCENARIO: Billy had a warrant for his arrest for Petit Theft. Officer Bob sees Billy walking down the street. Officer Bob checked his computer and saw that the warrant was active for Billy's arrest. He stops Billy and informs him that there was a warrant for his arrest. He tells Billy to turn around so he can handcuff him. Billy turns around and then Kicks Officer Bob in the Stomach and runs. Can Billy be Charged with Resisting Arrest with Violence? **YES.**

843.08 False personation A person who falsely assumes or pretends to be a firefighter, a sheriff, an officer of the Florida Highway Patrol, an officer of the Fish and Wildlife Conservation Commission, an officer of the Department of Environmental Protection, a fire or arson investigator of the Department of Financial Services, an officer of the Department of Financial Services, an officer of the Department of Corrections, a correctional probation officer, a deputy sheriff, a state attorney or an assistant state attorney, a statewide prosecutor or an assistant statewide prosecutor, a state attorney investigator, a coroner, a police officer, a lottery special agent or lottery investigator, a beverage enforcement agent, a school guardian as described in s. 30.15(1)(k), a security officer licensed under chapter 493, any member of the Florida Commission on Offender Review or any administrative aide or supervisor employed by the commission, any personnel or representative of the Department of Law Enforcement, or a federal law enforcement officer as defined in s. 901.1505, and takes upon himself or herself to act as such, or to require any other person to aid or assist him or her in a matter pertaining to the duty of any such officer, commits a felony of the third degree, punishable as provided in s. 775.082, s. 775.083, or s. 775.084. However, a person who falsely personates any such officer during the course of the commission of a felony commits a felony of the second degree, punishable as provided in s. 775.082, s. 775.083, or s. 775.084. If the commission of the felony results in the death or personal injury of another human being, the person commits a felony of the first degree, punishable as provided in s. 775.082, s. 775.083, or s. 775.084.

Read (False Impersonating). This Statute reviews the Offense of False Impersonation of a law Enforcement Officer or Governmental Official or Governmental Employee with Authority.

SCENARIO: Billy gets a set of Red and Blue Flashing Lights in his truck. Billy decides that he wants to pretend he is a Law Enforcement Officer and uses the flashing lights on his car to stop vehicles on Interstate 4. When Billy engages his lights, Cars start to pull over the drivers believe him to be a law Enforcement Officer with Authority.   Can Billy be Charged with False Personation of a Law Enforcement Officer? **YES.** Billy took not only placing Lights that resemble law Enforcement Authority he acted with them causing others to believe he was a Law Enforcement Officer.

843.081   Prohibited use of certain lights/penalty

(1)   The Legislature finds and declares that Florida's citizens are vulnerable to becoming the victims of criminal acts through the illegal use of blue lights by the criminal elements. It is the intent of the Legislature to reduce this vulnerability to injury and loss of life and property by prohibiting the use of certain blue lights by any person other than an authorized law enforcement officer.

(2)   It is unlawful for a person to use in or on any non-governmentally owned vehicle or vessel any flashing or rotating blue light unless such person is a law enforcement officer employed by a federal, state, county, or city law enforcement agency or is a person appointed by the Governor pursuant to chapter 354.

(3)   The provisions of this section shall not apply to salespersons, service representatives, or other employees of businesses licensed to sell or repair law enforcement equipment.

(4)   For the purposes of this section, the term "**flashing or rotating blue light**" includes

all forms of **lights** which display a blue light source or which were designed with the intent of displaying a blue light source whether or not such light is actually in use.

(5) Any person who violates any of the provisions of this section commits a misdemeanor of the first degree, punishable as provided in s. 775.082 or s. 775.083.

Read (Prohibited use of Certain Lights). This Statute reviews certain lights that are prohibited to use by Non-Law Enforcement and certain Governmental Entities and Persons.

In Florida the usage and emitting of a BLUE or RED light from any Vehicle or Vessel, is reserved for Law Enforcement Entities and Governmental agencies with AUTHORITY. Any Persons or Company that allows, authorizes, and uses Blue or Red emitting lighting from their vehicle, and or vessel is in Violation of this Statue and can be charged Criminally as outlined above.

843.085 Unlawful use of badges or other indicia of authority

(1)   It is unlawful for any person, unless appointed by the Governor pursuant to chapter 354, authorized by the appropriate agency, or displayed in a closed or mounted case as a collection or exhibit, to wear or display any authorized indicia of authority, including any badge, insignia, emblem, identification card, or uniform, or any colorable imitation thereof, of any federal, state, county, or municipal law enforcement agency, or other criminal justice agency as defined in s. 943.045, with the intent to mislead or cause another person to believe that he or she is a member of that agency or is authorized to display or wear such item, or to wear or display any item that displays in any manner or combination the word or words "police," "patrolman," "agent," "sheriff," "deputy," "trooper," "highway patrol," "commission officer," "Wildlife Officer," "Department of Environmental Protection officer," "Marine Patrol Officer," "state attorney," "public defender," "marshal,"

"constable," "bailiff," or "fire department," with the intent to mislead or cause another person to believe that he or she is a member of that agency or is authorized to wear or display such item.

Read (Unlawful use of Badges or other Identification). This Statute reviews the Unlawful use of Badges and other indicia of Authority.

SCENARIO: Billy buys a 5-Pointed Star Badge from an Army Navy Store. Billy sees two women arguing in a shopping plaza.   He walks up to both women and Flashes the badge and states that he is a Sheriff's Deputy and they both need to stop arguing and show him their ID's, or they will be arrested. Can Billy be Charged with Unlawful use of a Badge? **YES**. Could he also be charged with False Impersonating a LEO? **YES.**

CHAPTER 856
DRUNKENNESS/ OPEN HOUSE PARTIES/
LOITERING/PROWLING/DESERTION

856.011   Disorderly intoxication

(1)   No person in the state shall be intoxicated and endanger the safety of another person or property, and no person in the state shall be intoxicated or drink any alcoholic beverage in a public place or in or upon any public conveyance and cause a public disturbance.

(2)   Any person violating the provisions of this section shall be guilty of a misdemeanor of the second degree, punishable as provided in s. 775.082 or s. 775.083.

(3)   Any person who shall have been convicted or have forfeited collateral under the provisions of subsection (1) three times in the preceding 12 months shall be deemed a habitual offender and may be committed by the court to an appropriate treatment resource for a period of not more than 60 days. Any peace

officer, in lieu of incarcerating an intoxicated person for violation of subsection (1), may take or send the intoxicated person to her or his home or to a public or private health facility, and the law enforcement officer may take reasonable measures to ascertain the commercial transportation used for such purposes is paid for by such person in advance. Any law enforcement officers so acting shall be considered as carrying out their official duty.

Read (Disorderly Intoxication). This Statute reviews the Offense of Disorderly Intoxication.

SCENARIO: Billy has gotten really drunk and decided that he was going to walk down the street and into an intersection and start directing Traffic. Billy is causing drivers to swerve around him, and traffic was backing up in all directions. You contact Billy who smells of the impurities of an Alcoholic Beverage and he is yelling and refusing to get out of the road. He yells that he has had 15 drinks of jack Daniels and he does not need to listen to you. Can Billy be charged with Disorderly Intoxication? YES. Billy's actions were a direct threat to persons and property.

856.021   Loitering or prowling; penalty

(1)   It is unlawful for any person to loiter or prowl in a place, at a time or in a manner not usual for law-abiding individuals, under circumstances that warrant a justifiable and reasonable alarm or immediate concern for the safety of persons or property in the vicinity.

(2)   Among the circumstances which may be considered in determining whether such alarm or immediate concern is warranted is the fact that the person takes flight upon appearance of a law enforcement officer, refuses to identify himself or herself, or manifestly endeavors to conceal himself or herself or any object. Unless flight by the person or other circumstance makes it impracticable, a law enforcement officer shall, prior to any arrest for an offense under this section, afford the person an opportunity to dispel any alarm or immediate concern which would otherwise be warranted by requesting the person to identify himself or herself and explain his or her presence and conduct. No person shall be convicted of an offense under this section if the law

enforcement officer did not comply with this procedure or if it appears at trial that the explanation given by the person is true and, if believed by the officer at the time, would have dispelled the alarm or immediate concern.

(3) Any person violating the provisions of this section shall be guilty of a misdemeanor of the second degree, punishable as provided in s. 775.082 or s. 775.083.

Read (Loitering or Prowling). This Statute reviews the Offense of Loitering and Prowling. This Offense is something that you will deal with on a regular basis.

SCENARIO: Officer Bob is on Patrol. He is working the 10pm to 6am shift. As he is driving past a local shopping Plaza, he sees an **Unknown White Male looking into the closed businesses Windows and pulling on their front doors**. It is **3:30am in the Morning**. Officer Bob drives his **Marked Patrol Car** into the plaza towards the unknown white male. The unknown male **sees Officer Bob and starts to run and hides behind a dumpster** behind the building. Officer Bob goes after the male and calls him out from behind the dumpster. The white male steps out and tells Officer Bob that he wasn't doing anything. He has no Identification on him. He does not work at any of the Businesses there and advises that he doesn't live in the area. Can this person be Charged with Loitering and Prowling? YES. Read the Statue and look at the highlighted areas above.

This person was in an area where there were closed businesses and not at a time that normal patronage would be occurring. He is looking into the closed businesses windows and PULLING on the doors. Upon sight of Law Enforcement, (Officer Bob), this person ran and hide.

856.031   Arrest without warrant Any sheriff, police officer, or other law enforcement officer may arrest any suspected loiterer or prowler without a warrant in case delay in procuring one would probably enable such suspected loiterer or prowler to escape arrest.

Read (Arrest without warrant). This Statute reviews the Authority of Law Enforcement to make an arrest **without a warrant** needing to be issued, if he or she feels they have an individual or individuals detained for Loitering and Prowling.

CHAPTER 876

CRIMINAL ANARCHY/ TREASON/AND OTHER CRIMES AGAINST PUBLIC ORDER

876.12   Wearing mask, hood, or other device on public way No person or persons over 16 years of age shall, while wearing any mask, hood, or device whereby any portion of the face is so hidden, concealed, or covered as to conceal the identity of the wearer, enter upon, or be or appear upon any lane, walk, alley, street, road, highway, or other public way in this state.

Read (Wearing mask, hood or another device on **Public Roadway**). This Statute reviews the Offense of someone wearing a mask or hood or other device to conceal their face and identity.

SCENARIO: ANTIFA members decide to walk downtown Orlando wearing masks and hoods covering their faces and identities. They walk on the sidewalks Infront of Buildings on Orange Avenue. They start yelling and chanting blocking the sidewalk and roadway.   Officer Bob walks up and tells them all to remove their masks, and they all refuse. Can they all be charged Criminally for Violating this Statue? **YES**

876.13   Wearing mask/ hood, or other device on public property No person or persons shall in this state, while wearing any mask, hood, or device whereby any portion of the face is so hidden, concealed, or covered as to conceal the identity of the wearer, enter upon, or be, or appear upon or within the public property of any municipality or county of the state.

Read (Wearing mask, hood or another device on **Public property**). This Statute reviews the Offense of someone wearing a mask or hood or other device to conceal their face and identity.

SCENARIO: ANTIFA members decide to walk downtown Orlando wearing masks and hoods covering their faces and identities. They walk into the Local Park Next to Lake Eola. They start yelling and chanting blocking the public park walkways and entry to the Children's Park. Officer Bob walks up and tells them all to remove their masks, and they all refuse. Can they all be charged Criminally with Violating this Statue? **YES**

876.14   Wearing mask/ hood, or other device on property of another No person or persons over 16 years of age shall, while wearing a mask, hood, or device whereby any portion of the face is so hidden, concealed, or covered as to conceal the identity of the wearer, demand entrance or admission or enter or come upon or into the premises, enclosure, or house of any other person in any municipality or county of this state.

Read (Wearing mask, hood or another device on **Property of Another**). This Statute reviews the Offense of someone wearing a mask or hood or other device to conceal their face and identity.

SCENARIO: ANTIFA members decide to walk downtown Orlando wearing masks and hoods covering their faces and identities. They walk into a local neighborhood to a local politician's home. They start yelling and chanting blocking the Driveway. They also walk onto the front lawn with banners and are yelling at the occupants in the home to come out. Officer Bob walks up and tells them all to remove their masks, and they all refuse. Can they all be charged Criminally for Violating this Statue? **YES**

876.43   Unlawful entry on property Any individual, partnership, association, corporation, municipal corporation or state or any political subdivision thereof engaged in, or preparing to engage in, the manufacture, transportation or storage of any product to be used in the preparation of the United States, or of any country with which the United States shall then maintain friendly relations, or of any of the states for defense or for war or in the prosecution of war by the United States, or the manufacture, transportation, distribution or storage of gas, oil, coal, electricity or water, or any of said natural or artificial persons operating any public utility, whose property, except where it fronts on water or where there are entrances for railway cars, vehicles, persons or things, is surrounded by a fence or wall, or a fence or wall and buildings, may post around her or his or its property at each gate, entrance, dock or railway entrance and every 100 feet of waterfront a sign reading "No Entry Without Permission." Whoever without permission of such owner shall willfully enter upon premises so posted shall be guilty of a misdemeanor of the second degree, punishable as provided in s. 775.082 or s. 775.083.

Read (Unlawful entry on Property). This Statute reviews the Offense of someone Entering Property.

This statue touches on persons entering Posted Lands/or facilities which are Gated, Walled, Railroad Entrances, Railway Cars, Public Utility facilities, Oil, Coal and Gas Facilities, must post signage that is Visible at all gated entrances and Railway Entrances "No Entry Without Permission", and persons enter without permission are guilty of a misdemeanor of the second degree.

876.44   Questioning and detaining suspected persons Any peace officer or any other person employed as a person who watches or guards or in a supervisory capacity on premises posted as provided in s. 876.43 may stop any person found on any premises to which entry without permission is forbidden by s. 876.43 and may detain the person for the purpose of demanding, and may demand, of the person, his or her name, address and business in such place. If said peace officer or employee has reason to believe from the answers of the person so interrogated that such person has no right to be in such place, said peace officer shall forthwith release such person or he or she may arrest such person without a warrant on the charge of violating the provisions of s. 876.43, and said employee shall forthwith release such person or turn him or her over to a peace officer, who may arrest the person without a warrant on the charge of violating the provisions of s. 876.43.

Read (Questioning and detaining suspects). This Statute reviews the Right of a law Enforcement Officer, Security Officer, Security Guard, or Manager of a Facility and Posted property, the Right to Detain any persons whom they believed made entry onto Property without permission. Should a Security Officer Detain, they must immediately turn the detained person(s) over to law Enforcement. Same if persons were detained by Manager or Supervisor of said property.

SCENARIO: Billy and Joey hop a fenced in an area of a local warehouse in their neighborhood. The hired Security Officer/Guard makes contact with them. Can the Security Officer/Guard Detain the two? YES. Can the Security Officer/Guard use Controlling Force to detain them? YES. Can the property Manager or Supervisor Detain them? YES. Can they use Controlling Force to Detain them? YES.

148

Common Sense and Good Judgment Must be used.

CHAPTER 877
MISCELLANEOUS CRIMES

877.02   Solicitation of legal services or retainers therefor/ penalty.

(1)   It shall be unlawful for any person or her or his agent, employee or any person acting on her or his behalf, to solicit or procure through solicitation either directly or indirectly legal business, or to solicit or procure through solicitation a retainer, written or oral, or any agreement authorizing an attorney to perform or render legal service, or to make it a business to solicit or procure such business, retainers or agreements; provided, however, that nothing herein shall prohibit or be applicable to banks, trust companies, lawyer reference services, legal aid associations, lay collection agencies, railroad companies, insurance companies and agencies, and real estate companies and agencies, in the conduct of their lawful businesses, and in connection therewith and incidental thereto forwarding legal matters to

attorneys at law when such forwarding is authorized by the customers or clients of said businesses and is done pursuant to the canons of legal ethics as pronounced by the Supreme Court of Florida.

(3)   Any person violating any provision of this section shall be guilty of a misdemeanor of the first degree, punishable as provided in s. 775.082 or s. 775.083.

Read (Solicitation of Legal Services or Retainers) This Statute reviews the Offense of someone Solicitation legal services for themselves or another.

This statue touches on several things. Central Florida is rated #1 for Lawyer Commercials in the Nation. This means there is more T.V, Radio, Billboards, Mailings, Internet Commercials for Solicitation of Legal Services than anywhere else.   Now in the past, Lawyers were **not** allowed to solicit in the ways they do today.

SCENARIO: John the Lawyer needs Business and hangs out by a local Hospital. Whenever he sees an ambulance come in, he sneaks in to contact the injured person to see if they want his legal Services, and solicits the person requesting a retainer for his services. This is a violation of this statue, the term used for Lawyers who had used this method in the past and still do, is called an "Ambulance Chaser".

SCENARIO: Officer Bob is good friends with John the Injury Lawyer. Officer Bob is on a traffic crash scene and gives a victim at the scene John the Injury Lawyers Business card and tells the victim in the crash to call John the Lawyer for help. This is a Violation of this statue. Officer Bob cannot Solicit legal services for his Friend.

877.03   Breach of the peace/ disorderly conduct Whoever commits such acts as are of a nature to corrupt the public morals, or outrage the sense of public decency, or affect the peace and quiet of persons who may witness them, or engages in brawling or fighting, or engages in such conduct as to constitute a breach of the peace or disorderly conduct, shall be guilty of a misdemeanor of the second degree, punishable as provided in s. 775.082 or s. 775.083.

Read (Breach of Peace/Disorderly Conduct). This Statute reviews the Offense of Breaching the peace of others or Conduct Infront of others that disturbs the peace and quiet of another or Offend another by their conduct.

SCENARIO: John and Billy are at the Local Park enjoying a live Music Concert with their Families. While standing their watching the show, two unknown adult males start arguing with each other and then start to fight with each other. This fight stops the concert and John and Billy's, children see the fighting as both men started to yell and curse each other while fist fighting. Both John and Billy are outraged by these two individual's behaviors. There fight disrupted the concert and all those who was attending. Officer Bob Pulls up and stops the men from Fighting. John and Billy want to file a complaint and agree to be witnesses and victims to this offense. Can this be Disorderly Conduct? **YES.** Can both adult males who were fighting be charged? **YES**.

SURPRESSION HEARING

When it comes to a Law Enforcement Officer and dealing with the courts or I should say having to go to court to defend their investigation or their actions in a certain case or in reference to an arrest of a person or persons, they were involved in or was the primary officer in Charge, that Officer needs to remember the term **SURPRESSION HEARING.**

When you see a Law Enforcement Officer constantly going to court, it is usually because they have **poorly written reports**. I have had students in past classes that I Instructed would tell me that Officer Bob was in here in class yesterday and told us that he has a lot of Experience in Court because he says he's there all the time for his reports.   Well one thing I had to advise to the Class that if Officer Bob is constantly going to court to defend his reports, there is a good chance that Officer Bob writes reports that make Defense Attorneys smile.

I would say that **99%** of Suppression hearings that a law Enforcement Officer is Subpoenaed to attend, is usually a complaint that the Officer violated a suspect's **4th Amendment Rights**. This process is done by a Defense Attorney challenging the circumstances that the Law Enforcement Officer arrested their client or issues with probable cause or discovery the Officer used in obtaining a confession, or statement from their Client, this is done prior to a Trial and brought before a Judge to suppress certain evidence that a Defense Attorney feels was either obtained illegally or by improper processes by the Law Enforcement Officer.

In layman's terms, the Defense Attorney is trying to get either the whole case or certain evidence tossed prior to trial.

DON'T BE LIKE OFFICER BOB!

"Write Your Initial Reports as If an "Attorney" was writing IT"

WAIVER OF PROSECUTION

I want to touch on a Form that all Florida Law Enforcement Agencies have regarding "Waivers of Prosecution". The waiver of prosecution is a form that was designed to allow an alleged victim to a crime the ability to sign a Waiver of Prosecution for the Person or persons who allegedly committed a crime against them, to be sent to the State Attorney's Office for Consideration, so the State Attorney would not follow through with Formal Charges against the Suspect(s), Or I could say to stop any further prosecution against the Suspect(s). Some Law Enforcement Agencies think that if a Waiver is Signed, they can just walk away and let the suspect go. I saw this happen at an Agency where a Victim was stabbed in the throat. The Investigating Officers and Detective on Scene **allowed the victim** who was conscious to sign a waiver. They then let the Suspect walk, because the Victim Signed the Waiver. This was very carless and negligent of the Investigating Officers and Detective. This person was brutally stabbed in the throat. He was afraid of the Suspect and told the Officers and Detective he wanted to sign a waiver. You must understand, that a "Waiver of Prosecution", is only a form that is ***ASKING*** the State Attorney **not to prosecute further**. That decision ultimately is up to the Sate Attorney's Office whether a waiver is signed or not. The stabbing Victim in my above Scenario should not have had a waiver of prosecution waived in his face. **EVEN** with the Waiver Signed, that Suspect **should have been arrested**, for the type of Crime that was committed. The Officers and Detective could have made the Arrest and just sent a copy of the waiver with the Arrest Affidavit. A Waiver doesn't give a suspect a free pass to walk away from a crime scene and not have to be Arrested and processed.

DEDICATION

This book is dedicated to all the Men and Women in Florida Law Enforcement Today, and to those who have Served and Protected their Communities in the past

And to the people who had Motivated me Every Day to Put on a Uniform and Gun belt

James Walter Freeman Sr. and James Walter Freeman Jr., the Best Men I have ever known!!, who will never be forgotten!!

And to Arleen Freeman, Marie, Joshua, Sara, Brian, Darren and Emma.

Special Thanks to:

Haines City Police Department, Haines City Florida

Osceola County Sheriff's Office, Osceola County Florida

Davenport Police Department, Davenport Florida

The Criminal Justice Academy of Osceola (TECO)

"The Three Men who instilled what being a Law Enforcement Officer was to me"

"Jonny Perkins, Joe Johnson and Fred Casler"
(TECO)

Polk State College

South Florida State College

Valencia College

Law Enforcement and understanding State
Statues, County Ordinances, or City Ordinances
is something that every person who resides in
the State of Florida should have some
education and knowledge of.

Book Reference/Research Material for all
Florida State Statues, the Florida Legislature.

"KNOWLEDGE IS NOT POWER, APPLIED
KNOWLEDGE IS"

Darren W. Freeman